Catch
of the day

Catch
of the day

Marjie Lambert

CB
CONTEMPORARY BOOKS

Library of Congress Cataloging-in-Publication Data
is available from the United States Library of Congress.

A Quintet Book

This book was designed and produced by
Quintet Publishing Limited
6 Blundell Street
London N7 9BH

Creative Director: Richard Dewing
Art Director: Simon Daley
Design: Paul Wright
Editor: Debbie Foy
Photographer: Paola Zucchi
Food Stylist: Julz Beresford

Typeset in Great Britain by Central Southern Typesetters, Eastbourne
Manufactured in Hong Kong by Regent Publishing Services Ltd.

Published by Contemporary Books
A division of NTC/Contemporary Publishing Group, Inc.
4255 West Touhy Avenue, Lincolnwood (Chicago), Illinois 60646-1975 U.S.A.
Printed in China by Lee Fung Asco Printers Ltd.
International Standard Book Number: 0-8092-9917-8

99 00 01 02 03 04   19 18 17 16 15 14 13 12 11 10 9 8 7 6 5 4 3 2 1

PUBLISHER'S NOTE
Because of the slight risk of salmonella, raw eggs should not be served to the very young,
the ill or the elderly, or to pregnant women.

Contents

Although still not as high as island nations where it is the mainstay of the diet – such as Iceland, where the average person eats 63 pounds of seafood a year, or Japan, where the average consumption is 46 pounds – seafood consumption in the western world has come a long way from the days when fish sticks, deep-fried shrimp and fish fillets, and canned tuna were the only seafood that most people ate. The demand for fresh seafood has increased dramatically and stores are now stocking a greater variety than ever before, in response to customers' eagerness to sample different kinds of fish and their enthusiasm for learning how to cook it.

A world of fish

Seafood caters to the most Spartan of tastes as well as the most gourmet. It can be rich and served with a buttery sauce, or simply poached in an herb-flavored fish broth. Even ugly seafood that people formerly shunned, such as squid, monkfish, and catfish, are now prized and feature in many delectable dishes.

During the 1990s, 100 million metric tons of seafood were harvested from the world's oceans every year – double the annual catch of the mid-1960s – and a further 20 million metric tons were produced by aquaculture or fish farming. The average person in the United States and Canada consumed 15 to 16 pounds of seafood a year over this period, 50 percent more than in 1960. Seafood is now supplying our diet with an increasing amount of protein. Fish are good sources of vitamins B6 and B12; most are low in fat and those with a higher fat content are sources of healthful omega-3 fatty acids. Quite apart from the obvious benefits to our health in eating more fish, seafood is, quite simply, delicious.

No longer intimidated by buying and cooking seafood, we have learned how to recognize fresh fish that has a healthy smell of the sea and we have discovered that it can be one of the simplest of all foods to prepare. Most fish and shellfish are so versatile they can be baked, broiled, barbecued, steamed, fried, or poached. We have learned not to overcook it and how to complement it with a simple sauce, salsa, or butter to really bring out the flavor. Shellfish is a perennial favorite, particularly shrimp, clams, crab, and scallops, all easy to prepare and tempting to eat.

We love our home-grown crab – king crab in Alaska and western Canada, Dungeness in California and the Pacific Northwest, blue crabs in Maryland and the eastern seaboard, stone crabs in Florida – each of us swearing that our local crab is the best of all. We test our mettle by eating raw oysters, and turn to lobster to mark a special occasion.

The most popular seafood in the west is tuna, shrimp, pollock, salmon, cod, catfish, clams, crab, flounder/sole, halibut, and scallops. With the demand for seafood rising and some supplies being depleted, the fishing industry is increasingly relying on aquaculture to supplement what it can catch in the wild. Most of the world's aquaculture production is in Asia, where consumption of seafood is higher than in the western world. Salmon is farmed in Norway, Chile, and the United Kingdom. Ecuador is one of the biggest producers of farmed shrimp, and France and Spain are major shellfish producers. Australia pen-raises bluefin tuna. The United States ranks fifth in the world's aquaculture production, producing large amounts of clams, salmon, trout, catfish, and red snapper. This, in turn, is introducing consumers to fish that until fairly recently were available only regionally. A generation ago, for example, catfish was rarely eaten outside the southern United States. Now it is available in fish markets across the country. When Cajun restaurants began to serve blackened redfish, it quickly became the rage across America, to the point that supplies were depleted and the government was obliged to restrict redfish catches.

We hope this book will introduce you to new ways of preparing seafood and tempt you to try varieties you have not tried before. To entice you further, we have suggested wines and side dishes to accompany each recipe. We hope you will enjoy these recipes, and feel confident to alter them to suit your taste and try them with different kinds of fish.

Welcome to the wonderful world of seafood.

What to look for when buying seafood

Finding a reputable seafood seller with a knowledgeable staff, whether a fish market or a supermarket, is the single most important step in buying quality seafood. Ask friends, neighbors, and co-workers for recommendations. Look for signs of quality: consistently fresh seafood, no strong fishy or ammonia odors, staff who can competently answer questions about different types of seafood and their preparation.

Seafood – and seafood stores – should smell like the ocean. A strong fishy odor or the smell of ammonia means the fish is old. Avoid buying prepackaged fish – you can't smell it and judge the elasticity of the flesh.

Whole fish should have flesh that is firm and elastic. Pressed with the finger, it should spring back. The skin should be shiny, with the scales tightly attached. Gills should be bright pink or red. If they are green, gray, brown, or slimy, the fish is old. The eyes of most fish should be bright and clear; if the eyes are cloudy or sunken, this is another sign that the fish is old. The exception to this is deep-water fish such as tuna and mackerel. Bringing them up quickly from the deep can damage their eyes. Fillets and steaks should look and smell fresh and moist, with no dried-out surfaces or discoloration.

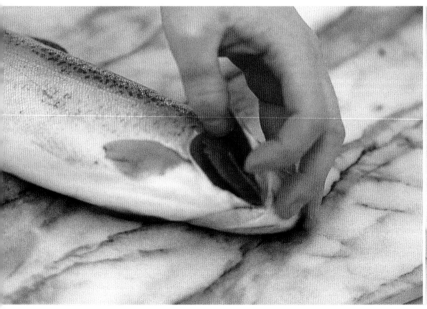

Frozen fish should be solidly frozen, tightly wrapped in moisture-proof packaging, with no freezer burns or signs of deterioration. When buying oysters, clams, and mussels, look for shells that are tightly closed or that close readily when you tap them sharply. Shucked oysters should be plump, have a creamy color, and be surrounded by clear liquid.

Fresh shrimp should have firm flesh. Most of the shrimp we buy has been previously frozen then defrosted, so the flesh is no longer as firm as it would have been originally. Wherever possible, buy shrimp that is still solidly frozen so you can defrost it at your convenience. Live crabs, lobsters, and crawfish should be active, not lethargic. Because they are highly perishable, scallops are almost never sold in the shell, but are shucked and gutted before selling. They should smell faintly sweet and look moist and gleaming. Their color will vary, depending on their diet, but they should not be snow-white – that indicates they have been soaked in water and weigh more than they should. Squid should have ivory-colored flesh visible beneath its outer, speckled covering. Yellowing flesh means the squid is old.

Eating raw seafood

You need to be very careful when buying seafood and preparing it for dishes in which it is to be eaten raw, such as seviche, sushi, and oysters, or dishes where the fish is barely cooked, such as seared tuna. The reason is that there may be bacteria and viruses in the water. The threat of bacteria is highest during warm summer months, which is why you often hear warnings against eating oysters harvested in May, June, July, and August. Shellfish beds are usually closed to harvesting when bacteria levels are high, but that is still no guarantee that any shellfish you buy are bacteria free. It is therefore extremely important to buy from a reputable fish merchant or store who will answer your questions about their produce, where it was caught, and how to store it.

Cooking kills bacteria, but there is a risk in eating raw or partially cooked seafood. It should be avoided by people with chronic liver disease, compromised immune systems or certain other health problems. Using frozen seafood will reduce the risk, although you may lose out on taste and texture. Making sure that shellfish were legally harvested from regulated growing beds also reduces the risk.

Storing fish

Seafood can usually be kept for a day or two at home, and very fresh fish can be stored, unfrozen, for several days, but it needs to be kept very cold. Seafood should be stored packed in ice at about 32 degrees, but most refrigerators keep food at about 40 degrees. The fish should be wrapped so the flesh does not come into direct contact with the ice. Pack ice cubes or small ice packs around the seafood and put it in the coldest part of your refrigerator, usually the bottom shelf. If you store it for longer than a day, refresh it with fresh ice at least once a day. As the ice melts, it needs to drain away from the fish. The fish should not sit in a pool of water.

Live shellfish, including oysters, lobsters, mussels, and clams, should be refrigerated in well-ventilated containers or paper bags. They should not be stored in airtight containers or plastic bags and should not be kept in water. Any shellfish that die during storage should be discarded: do not eat them.

Cleaning and preparing seafood

Unless you catch your own fish, your fish merchant will usually clean whole fish before selling them. If you have to do it yourself, however, cleaning most fish is relatively simple.

The easiest way to gut a roundfish is through the belly. Using a thin, sharp knife, cut open the belly, starting at the anal opening and working up to the jaw. Don't insert the knife too deeply into the fish – you want to avoid cutting into the viscera. Pull out and discard the viscera. With your knife, puncture the blood pockets on either side of the backbone. Lift the gill cover and pull out the gills. Rinse the inside of the fish thoroughly under running water.

The viscera of flatfish take up only a small, forward part of the body cavity. If you want to leave the head on, make a small incision behind the gills, then pull out the viscera. Or you can cut off the head and viscera cavity altogether. In both cases, rinse the fish well.

To scale a fish, grasp it by the tail. Working from the tail to the head, scrape off the scales with a fish scaler or a serrated knife. Use short, firm strokes. If the fish skin is going to be removed after cooking or if the fish is going to be filleted, it does not have to be scaled.

To fillet a roundfish, cut off the pectoral and pelvic fins, but leave the anal and dorsal fins attached. Place the fish on its side with its backbone toward you. Make two shallow cuts from the top to the bottom of the fish at either end – at the tail end, where the meaty end turns into tail, and another one behind the gills. Working right next to the backbone, cut from head to tail, going all the way through the flesh to the backbone. Gently use your knife to separate the fillet from the bones and peel back the meat. Remove any bones from the fillet with tweezers. Then turn the fish over and repeat.

To fillet a flatfish, place the fish on a cutting board with the tail end toward you. Cut across the body below the gill and through to the bone. Do the same at the tail end. Then starting at the head, separate the flesh from the bones, using long, smooth strokes. Lift off the fillet. Turn over and repeat. For a larger flatfish, cut two fillets from each side by making a long cut the length of the fish, midway between the dorsal and anal fins. Trim edges and remove bones.

Lobster

To cook a whole, live lobster tie up and secure its claws tightly. To immobilize it, make a deep incision in the small cross-shaped depression at the top of the head (this is optional) then plunge the lobster into boiling water – the lobster will die within a few seconds. Allow 5 minutes for the first pound in weight, and 3 minutes for subsequent pounds. The lobster is done when the shell turns bright red.

To extract the meat you must first cut the lobster lengthwise in half through the shell. Make an incision in the tail to allow any residual boiling liquid to drain away then, holding the lobster flat, back upward, cut the tail in half lengthwise. Turn over the lobster and cut through the head. Remove and discard the inedible head sac then proceed to pick out the remaining, edible, meat. The liver (tomalley) is particularly prized. If you have a female lobster, include the coral. Twist off the legs and claws and extract their meat. Remove and discard the intestinal vein from the tail and extract the tailmeat. Discard the tail shell. Remove and discard the gills, known as "dead men's fingers," from the underside of the body shell. Pile all the lobster meat into this cleaned-out half shell to serve.

Crab

To boil a live crab, secure the claws with string and plunge into boiling water. The crab will die within a few seconds. Allow 5 minutes for the first pound in weight, and 3 minutes for subsequent pounds. To clean Dungeness and golden crabs, remove the back shell. Remove and discard the bile sac. Turn the crab on its back. Pull off and discard the rough triangle of shell and gray feathery gills known as "dead men's fingers." Rinse the center of the crab and remove the small white intestine. Blue and white crabs are too small to pick the meat for use in other recipes. To eat these crabs boiled, first twist off the claws and pick out the meat. You can pull off the

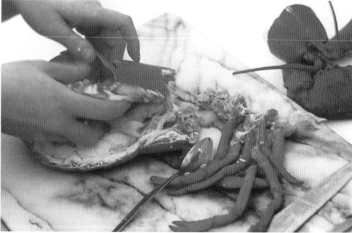

triangular shell and the top shell, then break the body and pick out the meat, or you can crack the body, shell and all, with a mallet, then pick out the meat.

Most other crabs, including king, snow, and stone crabs, are sold leg and claws-only, pre-boiled. Crack the claws with a mallet and pick out the meat.

Mussels and clams

Mussels and clams require very little work unless you collect them yourself. If you do, then you must purge them to rid them of all traces of sand and grit before cooking. Place them in a bucket of clear seawater or fresh water to which you've added a handful or two of salt – they will die in unsalted water

If you have cornmeal, add a handful to the water. Allow them to sit for about 20 minutes, then change the water and repeat at least twice.

The mussels' beards – the fibers by which they attach themselves to the pilings – must be pulled off. Mussels die soon after debearding, so don't remove the beards until just before cooking. Mussel and clam shells should be well-scrubbed with a stiff brush to remove sand and barnacles.

Mussels and clams are usually cooked in the shell. To remove them before cooking, however, pry open the shell with a knife and cut through the muscle that attaches them to the bottom shell.

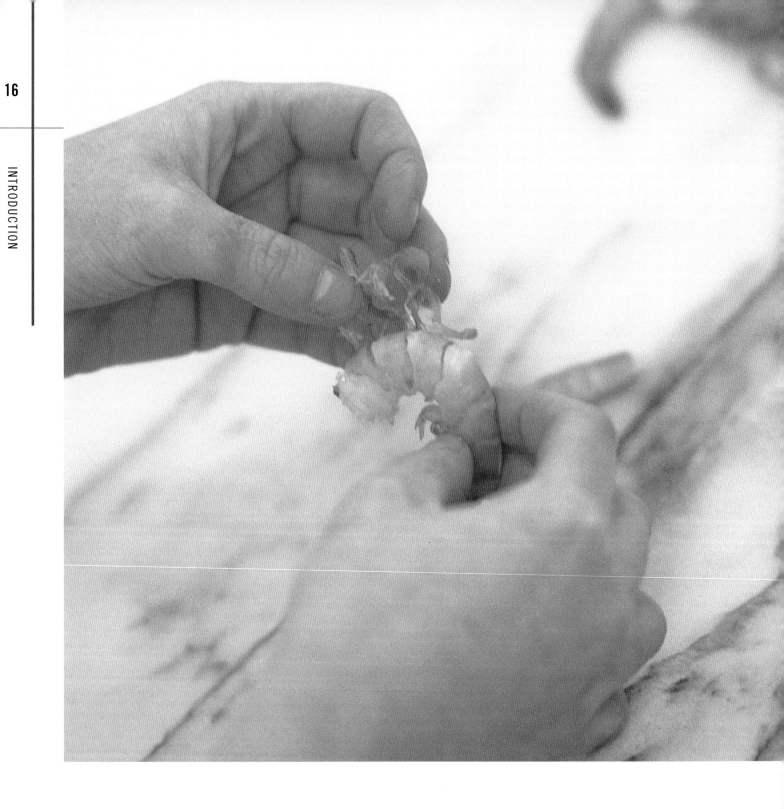

Shrimp

To clean shrimp, remove the shell and legs. You may leave the soft tail fins attached, if desired. To devein – especially in larger shrimp, where the vein tends to be gritty – make a shallow cut lengthwise down what looks like the back spine. Pull out the vein or wash it free. To clean whole shrimp, cut off the tail right behind the head.

Oysters

To shuck an oyster, protect your hand with heavy gloves, a potholder, or a towel. Cutting your hand with the sharp edge of an oyster shell is not only painful, but can cause an infection. Place the oyster on a flat surface with the deep, rounded side down. Find the hinge and insert the tip of an oyster knife between the top and bottom shells. Working carefully, pry the two shells slightly apart, then slide the oyster knife or a long slender blade between the oyster and top shell and sever the muscle that connects them. Carefully remove the top shell so that you don't lose any of the oyster liquid. Slide the knife under the oyster and carefully cut the firm muscle connecting it to the bottom shell.

Squid

Grasp the head of the squid where it enters the body and pull it off, pulling out as many innards as you can at the same time. Reach into the body – cut it open with a knife if you need to – and pull out the transparent quill-like cartilage and any remaining innards. Scrape out with a teaspoon if necessary. Discard the innards and cartilage. Rinse out the body and trim the wings. On larger squid, peel off the

speckled outer membrane; on small squid, the membrane is tender. Now clean the head: cut off the hard round beak and eyes and discard. Reserve the tentacles. For tiny squid, discard the whole head.

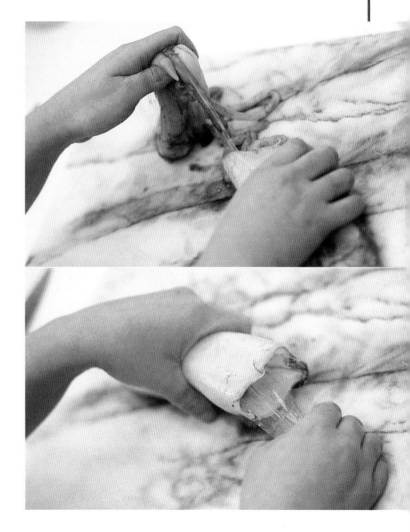

Cooking seafood

Grilling fish on a barbecue

This is an excellent way to cook sturdier fish, such as tuna and swordfish. Shellfish is particularly enhanced by the smoky flavor of a barbecue. Delicate fillets, such as flounder, cannot be grilled because they will fall apart during cooking. A fillet or steak with the skin still on will hold together better than skinned fish. Some fish that are difficult to cook on the grill can barbecued in a fish basket. For shrimp or other small items, consider using a grill tray with smaller holes (so shrimp don't fall through) or cooking them on skewers.

The barbecue is ready when the flames have died down and the coals are glowing and mostly covered with ash. Gas grills should be preheated. The grill should be cleaned and either the grill or the fish should be oiled (an oil-based marinade will do this job very well).

How long fish should cook depends on your taste and the heat of the barbecue, but a guideline is 6 to 12 minutes per inch of thickness. Steaks should be turned; thin fillets or small, butterflied fish, such as trout, should be cooked skin-side down and do not need to be turned. Fish should be cooked until the last bit of translucency remains in the center; it will continue to cook after it is removed from the heat.

Clams, mussels, and oysters should be scrubbed, then placed directly over the hot coals. Cook for 5 to 10 minutes, until the shells open. Shrimp can be grilled on a tray or skewers. Thread them loosely on a skewer: don't pack them tightly or they will cook unevenly. Leaving the shells on will help protect them from scorching. Cooking takes less than 5 minutes; shrimp overcook easily and become dry.

Broiling

Oven-broiling is easier and less messy than grilling. The heat is consistent and more easily controlled. Delicate fillets that can't be barbecued can be broiled although the broiler will not produce the smoky flavor or the seared crust that cooking on a barbecue does.

To broil unmarinated fish, season it with salt and pepper or your choice of seasonings, and brush it with a liquid such as lemon juice, wine, or olive oil. Set it on a lightly oiled broiler pan and put it under the preheated broiler. Thin fillets or small butterflied fish such as trout should be cooked skin-side down and can be placed close to the heating element. These will cook in 3 to 6 minutes and should not be turned. Thicker fillets and steaks should be placed further away from the heating element so the inside has time to cook before the top is too brown. Allow between 8 and 11 minutes in total per inch of thickness. Steaks should be turned once during cooking; most fillets do not need to be turned. Whole fish should not be too close to the broiler; they should be turned once.

Shrimp, lobster, crab, and scallops broil well but quickly – watch them closely. Oysters, clams, and mussels also can be broiled, but easily overcook and become tough, and there is little advantage to broiling over steaming or grilling them.

Pan-Frying/Sautéeing

Steaks, fillets, and small whole fish can be fried; among shellfish, shrimp and scallops are the best choice for frying. All can be fried plain – with no coating – or they can be dipped in flour, cornmeal, bread crumbs, or batter. The type and amount of fat used are a matter of preference. Butter adds more flavor but burns at a lower temperature than most vegetable oils. Among vegetable oils, peanut oil is best for frying at a very high temperature.

If you use a nonstick pan, you need only a small amount of fat, a teaspoon or two for frying, but you need a little for flavor and crust. If you don't want to use any fat, it is better to steam or poach the fish.

The skillet and cooking fat should be hot when you add the fish. A thin fillet will cook quickly, in as little as 3 to 4 minutes.

A 1-inch steak will take about 10 minutes, and a whole fish may take longer. Test the thickest part of the flesh – it is done when there is still a bit of transparency in the center. The fish will continue to cook after it is removed from the heat.

Deep-frying

Shrimp, oysters, clams, fillets, or strips of fish can be coated in batter and deep-fried. When done the outside is crisp and the inside succulent. The trick is to ensure the cooking oil is at the right temperature, which for most seafood is 365°F. If the oil is too hot, the outside will burn while the inside is raw. If it is not hot enough, the food will absorb a lot of extra oil, producing a soggy, greasy result. A thermometer is essential, and should be used almost constantly. The temperature of oil drops when food is added to it, so you need to bring it back up before you add another batch of fish. Once it reaches the right temperature, it continues to increase, climbing quickly to 400°F or hotter.

Fish or shellfish should be ready-coated in batter before you begin cooking. Heat the oil to 365°F in a deep skillet, wok, or pot. Using tongs, add several pieces of seafood taking care they do not crowd each other. Cook until golden brown, turning once, about 2 minutes for clams or shrimp, 3 minutes for oysters or small fillets, and a little longer for larger pieces. Remove and drain. Bring the oil back to 365°F before adding more fish.

Baking and Roasting

Because most seafood has a low fat content, it needs additional moisture when being cooked by dry heat. This can be melted butter or sauce drizzled over fish steaks, a little wine or fish broth for fillets wrapped in foil or cooked *en papillote*, or simply sealing in natural juices with foil or a tightly covered pan. Ovens vary in performance, but fish is usually baked at about 400°F, and the guideline of 7 to 10 minutes of cooking per inch of thickness usually applies. However, when fish is sealed in foil or a claypot has to rely on the enclosed moisture for braising, cooking times may be double or more.

Poaching and Steaming

Poaching and steaming are ideal ways of cooking many types of seafood. The fish won't dry out, it will absorb the flavor of the cooking liquid, and no fat is needed, so it is a healthy option. That does not mean that seafood can be neglected when being cooked in this way: seafood can toughen if overcooked by any method. Thin fillets are done in 5 to 8 minutes. A 1-inch thick halibut steak takes about 10 minutes. A 3-pound whole fish is steamed in 10 to 15 minutes.

In poaching, fish is immersed in liquid that simmers but does not boil. Using court-bouillon, wine or other seasoned liquid will impart the flavor to the fish. Firm-textured fish such as swordfish and salmon take well to poaching. High-fat, soft-textured fish such as bluefish or delicate fillets will simply fall apart. If you wrap the fish in cheesecloth, leaving long "handles" of cheesecloth at either end, you can lift the fish out of the poaching liquid easily.

Steaming, in which fish is cooked on a rack over – not in – boiling liquid has similar advantages. The water can be seasoned with spices, herbs, wine, onions, and other

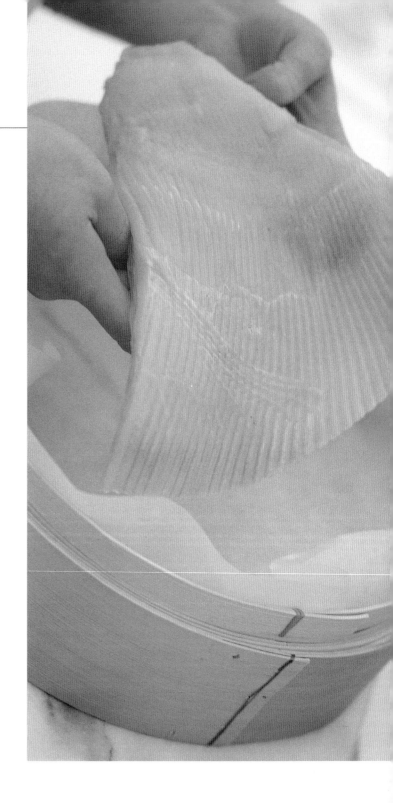

vegetables and will impart delicate flavors to the fish. Fillets that cannot be poached can be steamed. Mussels and clams are particularly good steamed, and are done when the shells open, about 5 to 10 minutes. Steamed blue crabs are done in about 20 minutes; Dungeness crabs may take twice as long.

Boiling

Except when added to soup, fish is almost never boiled. However, boiling is the simplest way of cooking shellfish. It's easy to ruin good shellfish by overcooking, so monitor closely. If it is being cooked in soup, remove the pot from the heat and serve the soup as soon as the seafood is done. If the seafood is being boiled in water and is not going to be eaten immediately or is going to be served cold, plunge it into ice water to stop the cooking process, then drain quickly. This is especially effective with shrimp.

If you are adding spices to the water in which shellfish are to be boiled, allow the spices to boil for about 15 minutes so the flavors can develop. The cooking time for crab depends on the size. Small blue crabs and rock crabs usually take about 5 minutes. Larger Dungeness and golden crabs will usually take 12 to 20 minutes and turn bright red when done.

Crawfish should be boiled 4 to 8 minutes, depending on their size, until they turn bright red and curl up. A 1-pound lobster takes about 6 to 8 minutes; a 3-pounder will take 10 to 15 minutes.

Oysters need very little cooking and are typically immersed in boiling liquid only when used in soup. Usually, the heat of a soup or gumbo that has just been removed from the stove is enough to cook oysters. Cook only until the edges begin to curl. An overcooked oyster will be leathery in texture and its delicate flavor will be lost.

To cook clams and mussels, bring water to a boil then lower the heat to a simmer before adding them. Cook until the shells open, 3 to 5 minutes for mussels and small clams, as much as 10 minutes for larger clams. When adding shelled clams and mussels to soups, reduce the heat. They will be cooked in 2 to 4 minutes. If you are making chowder with large, chopped clams, however, the clams may be simmered for up to an hour.

Scallops take less than 1 minute to cook in boiling liquid; they should be added after the heat is reduced. Boiled shrimp are done in 2 to 3 minutes, although jumbo shrimp take a little longer. Watch for the flesh to turn white and opaque and the bodies to curl tightly. Squid should be simmered for at least 30 minutes: it may take an hour or so for it to become tender.

Sauces and flavored butters add interest to seafood dishes and enhance the flavor of the fish. It is important to choose the right one, which will complement the fish rather than overwhelm it. Butters are easy to prepare and add a note of sophistication to seafood. They go well with delicately flavored fish, such as sole or cod, whereas spicy salsas bring out the strong flavors of meatier fish such as tuna and salmon. Hollandaise and mayonnaise are classic sauces which can partner many different kinds of seafood and provide a good base for a number of variations, such as Chive Hollandaise Sauce and Tartare Sauce. Some herbs, such as dill and tarragon, go extremely well with fish, as do some spices, notably saffron. Sauces, butters, and dressings in which they feature are guaranteed to add to the success of a seafood dish. Other, more unexpected ingredients, such as mango or lime, also appear in some of the sauces and butters in this section and add a novel touch. A good homemade fish broth provides a well-flavored basis for many soups and other seafood dishes which is infinitely superior in flavor and quality to any store-bought bouillon cube. The classic court-bouillon, flavored with vegetables, wine, and herbs, is the perfect poaching liquid for fish. Recipes for both are included in this section.

court-bouillon

Court bouillon is a seasoned liquid used for poaching fish. It typically consists of water and wine or wine vinegar, seasoned with herbs and vegetables such as onions and carrots. Here is one version.

TO COOK 6LB FISH
10 cups water
2 tsp salt
2 cups peeled and sliced
  carrots
2 cups peeled and sliced
  onions
¼ cup parsley stalks

4 Tbsp white wine or white
  wine vinegar
2 bouquets garnis or 2 bay
  leaves
Few sprigs thyme
6 peppercorns, slightly
  crushed

Place all the ingredients except the peppercorns in a fish kettle or large saucepan. Bring the liquid to a boil and skim to remove any surface residue.

Simmer for approximately 3 to 5 minutes then add the crushed peppercorns and continue simmering for a further 10 to 20 minutes. Allow to cool and strain thoroughly through a fine sieve.

Use as required. After cooking fish in the court-bouillon the broth can be used several times if strained each time.

To store, pour into a plastic bag or box, seal, and freeze until cooking fish again.

This amount is for large fish and may be halved for smaller quantities.

basic fish broth

Ask your fish merchant for about 3lb of fish bones, heads, and tails, from non-oily fish. Make sure the gills are removed, and that the fish trimmings are washed clean of any blood, and rinse under cold running water for several minutes.

2 Tbsp olive oil
2 onions, sliced
2 carrots, sliced
3 sticks celery, chopped

6 to 8 sprigs parsley
2 bay leaves
Fish trimmings

Heat the oil in a saucepan and sauté the onions, carrots, and celery for 10 minutes. Add the parsley, bay leaves, and fish trimmings, and enough water to cover by 1 inch.

Bring to a boil. Lower the heat and simmer, uncovered, for 25 minutes. Occasionally skim off any scum.

Pour the broth through a sieve and discard solids. Taste the broth and if it tastes weak, return it to the heat and simmer for a further 10 to 15 minutes.

aïoli

Aïoli is a rich and flavorful mayonnaise with puréed garlic cloves as a base. It comes from Provence in the south of France, where it is also sometimes known as "beurre de Provence." Aïoli can be made using bottled mayonnaise: crush the garlic and salt then gradually stir in the prepared mayonnaise.

6 to 12 cloves garlic, peeled
Salt and freshly ground black pepper
2 egg yolks (see page 4)
½ to 1 tsp Dijon mustard (optional)
About 1¼ cups olive oil
1½ Tbsp lemon juice or white wine vinegar,
   or a mixture of the two

Put the garlic cloves and a pinch of salt into a mortar or bowl and crush them together until reduced to a paste. Work in the egg yolks, and mustard if using.

Add the oil, a few drops at a time, while stirring slowly, evenly, and constantly to emulsify. After half the oil has been incorporated, add half the lemon juice or vinegar. The remaining oil can now be added in a more steady drizzle but continue to stir the sauce in the same way.

Add the remaining lemon juice or vinegar and season to taste.

Makes about 1½ cups

tartare sauce

This tangy sauce uses bottled mayonnaise as a base, but if you are comfortable with raw eggs (see page 4) use homemade mayonnaise and omit the olive oil and sour cream.

2 Tbsp olive oil
1 cup mayonnaise
2 Tbsp sour cream
1 Tbsp lemon juice
¼ cup chopped gherkins
1 Tbsp chopped capers

2 Tbsp fine chopped scallions
1 clove garlic, minced
½ tsp salt
¼ tsp black pepper

Place the mayonnaise in a small bowl and whisk in the olive oil until incorporated. Whisk in the sour cream, followed by the remaining ingredients. Chill for at least 2 hours to allow the flavors to blend.

chive hollandaise sauce

This is an easy way to make hollandaise sauce in the food processor. Adding the butter while it is still bubbling is critical – it will be hot enough to thicken the sauce but not so hot that it cooks the egg yolks.

4 egg yolks at room temperature (see page 4)
2 Tbsp lemon juice
1 Tbsp snipped chives

½ tsp salt
Pinch cayenne
1½ sticks unsalted butter

Put all the ingredients except the butter in the food processor, but do not process yet. Melt the butter over low heat until it is bubbling but not browned. Process the yolk mixture for 3 seconds, then with the motor running, slowly pour in the hot butter until it is all incorporated and the sauce is pale yellow and slightly thick. The butter must be taken directly from the heat to the processor; if it is allowed to cool even slightly, the sauce will not thicken.

Top tartare sauce
Bottom chive hollandaise sauce

velouté sauce

Velouté is a variation on white sauce, in which fish broth is substituted for milk. For a richer sauce, substitute ½ cup cream for an equal amount of the fish broth.

2 Tbsp butter
2 Tbsp flour
2 cups fish broth (page 26)

Salt and white pepper
Pinch nutmeg, optional

Melt the butter in a small pan. Add the flour and stir with a wooden spoon until it forms a smooth paste. Continue cooking for about 2 minutes, until the paste foams and the color is between ivory and pale yellow.

Gradually add the fish broth, stirring well so the sauce is smooth. Continue cooking until the sauce is thick enough to coat the back of a spoon. Whisk in the salt, white pepper, and, if desired, the nutmeg.

shallot herb dressing

This dressing goes well with seafood salads. It also makes a delicious marinade or basting sauce for fish.

1½ Tbsp lemon juice
½ cup extra-virgin olive oil
1 tsp Dijon mustard
1 tsp fine minced shallot

1½ tsp fresh herbs such as
  tarragon, chervil, or basil
1 tsp salt and a pinch pepper

Put all the ingredients in a jar or bottle and shake well.

warm citrus-mushroom salsa

This complements grilled or broiled fish and seafood or warm green vegetables, such as broccoli, Brussels sprouts, green beans, snow peas, and lima beans.

Heat the oil in a large skillet over medium heat. Add the shallots or scallions and cook for 1 minute. Add the mushrooms and cook for a few seconds to soften slightly.

Add orange juice and clam juice and bring to a boil. Simmer 5 to 7 minutes, until the mushrooms are tender. Uncover and boil over high heat until the liquid is slightly thickened, about 5 minutes.

Season with salt and pepper and stir in parsley or cilantro.

1 Tbsp olive oil
2 shallots, or white part of 4 scallions, peeled and minced
5½ cups fresh mushrooms, trimmed and thin sliced
½ cup orange juice
½ cup bottled clam juice
Salt and black pepper to taste
¼ cup chopped parsley or cilantro

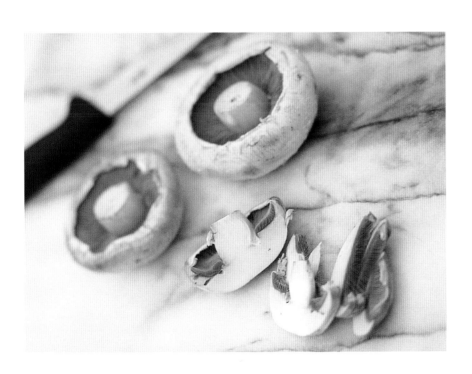

mango and red pepper salsa

Spicy fruit salsas are especially good with grilled or broiled fish. Substitute papayas for the mangoes for an equally delicious salsa. For a milder but still somewhat spicy salsa, remove the veins and seeds from the chiles. For a very hot salsa, substitute one habanero or Scotch bonnet chile (but protect your hands with gloves or a plastic bag).

2 ripe mangoes, peeled and diced
1 red bell pepper, diced
1 or 2 jalapeño or serrano chiles, minced
2 cloves garlic, chopped
Juice of 1 lime
¼ to ½ red onion, chopped
½ cup chopped cilantro
Pinch salt, if needed

Combine the mangoes with the red bell pepper, chiles, garlic, lime, red onion, and cilantro, and a good pinch of salt if needed.

Chill until ready to serve.

three-color salsa

This goes well with any fish or seafood dish, especially Lime-marinated Swordfish on Citrus Noodles (page 84).

Juice of 1 lime
2 ripe avocadoes, peeled and cut into bite-size chunks
4 cups cherry tomatoes, stemmed and quartered
5 cups frozen or canned corn kernels, drained
1 Tbsp olive oil
2 Tbsp chopped cilantro
¼ tsp minced garlic
Salt and black pepper to taste
Hot pepper sauce to taste (optional)
Papaya seeds (optional)

Squeeze the lime juice over the avocadoes. Toss the tomatoes and corn in olive oil. Combine the avocadoes with the tomato-corn mixture and season with cilantro, garlic, salt, pepper, and hot sauce. Sprinkle a few papaya seeds on top, if you like.

Far left mango and red pepper salsa
Top three-color salsa

mango butter

**If mangoes are unavailable, substitute 4 ounces
peach and 4 ounces pineapple puréed together.
Use to sauté Pecan-crusted Flounder (page 74).**

2 sticks butter, softened
8 oz fresh or canned mango,
    peeled or drained and
    puréed

2 tsp lime juice
2 Tbsp fine chopped mint
1 tsp grated nutmeg

Mash the softened butter with a fork and add the other
ingredients. Roll the mixture into a log and wrap in plastic
wrap. Refrigerate until ready to use.

Right mango butter
Far right saffron-orange butter

saffron-orange butter

Serve with lobster, scallops, or shrimp.

2 sticks butter, softened
Fine grated zest of 2 oranges

1 tsp powdered saffron

Soften the butter with a fork, and mix in the remaining
ingredients. Roll the mixture into a log and wrap in plastic
wrap. Refrigerate until needed.

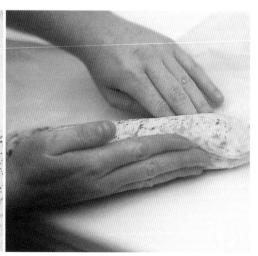

Seafood, on its own or partnered by roasted vegetables, herbs, cognac, or cream, lends itself particularly well to soup recipes and offers a wide range of possibilities, from smooth puréed soups which can be served as elegant appetizers to heartier, coarser-textured soups that are almost a stew, such as the San Francisco Cioppino. The flavor can be as delicate or spicy as you like, from the Shellfish Bisque to the Thai Hot and Sour Noodle Soup with Shrimp. Smoked fish also works particularly well in soups, as in Roasted Pumpkin and Smoked Mussel Soup and the Smoked Salmon Chowder. All it takes to turn these delicious soups into a perfect meal is a salad of ripe tomatoes and plenty of hot, crusty bread.

squid, tomato, and roasted bell pepper soup

Long, slow cooking tenderizes squid, so this recipe calls for it to be simmered in the soup for 60 minutes before the roasted bell pepper and more tomatoes are added. If juicy tomatoes are unavailable, substitute canned tomatoes.

Cut the squid open into two halves, then cut across into 1-inch slices.

Heat the oil in a large saucepan or small stockpot. Add the onions and garlic and cook until softened. Stir in half the tomatoes, the dried basil, 2 cups of fish broth, and the wine. Bring to a boil, then lower the heat. Add the squid, cover, and simmer for 1 hour.

Meanwhile, roast the red bell peppers. Cut each bell pepper into 3 or 4 nearly flat pieces. Place under a broiler, skin-side up. Cook until the skins are blistered and almost black. Remove from the broiler and place in a paper bag for at least 10 minutes. The skin will then peel off easily. Fine chop the roasted bell peppers.

When the soup has simmered for one hour, add the roasted bell peppers, the remaining chopped tomatoes, and fish broth. Continue cooking until the squid is tender, about 30 minutes. Add salt and pepper to taste. Ladle the soup into bowls and sprinkle with parsley or basil to serve.

2½ lb prepared squid
¼ cup olive oil
2 medium onions, fine chopped
2 cloves garlic, minced
2 lb ripe tomatoes, chopped
2 tsp dried basil
5 cups fish broth
½ cup red wine
2 red bell peppers
Salt and black pepper
1 Tbsp chopped parsley or basil, to garnish

Serves 4 to 6

Alternative fish: shrimp

Recommended wine: Zinfandel or Pinot Noir

Serving suggestion: salade niçoise with tarragon vinaigrette (page 90) or deep-fried oyster salad (page 96).

SOUPS

shellfish bisque

This is a classic Cajun soup made with crawfish, which are a staple in Louisiana cuisine. Most of the rich flavor in the broth comes from simmering the shells, but the shellfish meat is a delicious addition. This bisque uses only a pinch of cayenne and is not as spicy as some Cajun dishes.

Remove the shells and heads, if any, from the shrimp, reserving them for the broth. For crawfish, crab, or lobster, chop the shells in small pieces. Cover and chill the shellfish meat, either for use in the soup or for another purpose.

For the broth, heat the oil in a large pan over high heat. Add the shellfish shells and heads, if any, and sauté until they start to brown. Reduce the heat to medium and add the onion, carrot, and celery. Cook, stirring occasionally, for about 3 minutes, until the onion starts to soften. Add the water, lemon, and bouquet garni. Bring to a boil, reduce the heat to low, and simmer gently, partially covered, for 25 minutes. Strain the broth.

Melt the butter in a heavy pan over moderate heat. Stir in the flour and cook until slightly golden, stirring occasionally. Add the cognac and gradually pour in about half the broth, whisking vigorously until smooth, then add the remaining broth, still whisking. Season with cayenne (salt is not usually needed). Reduce the heat, cover, and simmer gently for about 5 minutes, stirring occasionally.

Strain the soup if not completely smooth. Add the cream and lemon juice to taste. Reheat the shellfish meat, if using, briefly in the soup before serving.

12 oz small cooked shrimp in the shell, or 1 lb with heads, or about 1½ lb hard-shelled shellfish, such as crawfish, crab, or lobster, cooked
2 Tbsp butter
4 Tbsp flour
2 Tbsp cognac
Pinch cayenne
4 to 5 Tbsp heavy cream
Lemon juice

BROTH
2 tsp vegetable oil
Shellfish shells and heads, or chopped small shellfish (about 1 lb)
1 onion, halved and sliced
1 small carrot, sliced
1 stick celery, sliced
4 cups water
½ lemon (unwaxed or scrubbed), sliced
1 bouquet garni (thyme sprigs, parsley, and bay leaf)

Serves 4

Recommended wine: Voignier, Gewürztraminer, Chardonnay.
Serving suggestion: Serve with a green salad, mixed with a selection of chopped vegetables, or with sandwiches of cheese, avocado, tomato, and sunflower seeds.

roasted pumpkin and smoked mussel soup

A luxurious soup that is good as a main course for a fall lunch or as a sophisticated appetizer.

Preheat the oven to 425°F. Cut the pumpkin into slices about 1½ to 2 inches wide and place them in a roasting pan. You will need 6 slices. Season lightly with pepper then brush the flesh with olive oil. Bake in the preheated oven for about 30 minutes, until the pumpkin is tender. Scoop the flesh from the skin and set aside until ready to use.

Heat 2 tablespoons of olive oil in a large pan; add the leek, celery, and carrot and cook slowly until soft. Stir in the coriander and cook slowly for a further minute. Add the pumpkin flesh to the pan with the thyme and bay leaf, then pour in the broth. Bring the soup to a boil then cover and simmer slowly for 35 to 40 minutes.

Allow the soup to cool slightly then purée until smooth in a blender or food processor. Rinse the pan then return the soup to it with the milk and bring slowly to simmering point. Season well with salt and pepper then add the smoked mussels and heat for another minute or two. Serve garnished with parsley.

½ small pumpkin or 1 medium firm-fleshed
   squash, about 1 lb
Black pepper
3 Tbsp olive oil
1 leek, fine sliced
2 sticks celery, trimmed and sliced
1 carrot, sliced
2 tsp coriander
3 to 4 sprigs thyme
1 bay leaf
3 cups well-flavored vegetable broth
2 cups milk
Salt
5 oz smoked mussels
Chopped parsley, to garnish

Serves 6

Alternative fish: smoked clams or smoked oysters.

Recommended wine: Sauvignon Blanc.

Serving suggestion: serve with multigrain bread and a salad of tomatoes, sweet onions, basil, and fresh mozzarella cheese.

thai hot and sour noodle soup with shrimp

This is one of the most exquisite dishes of Thai cuisine. The broth is a myriad of texture and flavors – sour lime leaves and lemon grass, spicy ginger and chiles, and sweet seafood. If you cannot obtain kaffir lime leaves, substitute 1 tablespoon fresh lime juice and lemon grass with 1 teaspoon grated lemon zest.

Heat the oil in a pan. When hot, stir-fry the garlic, shallots, ginger, and chiles for 1 minute. Pour in the broth, then add the lime leaves and lemon grass. Bring to a boil and simmer for 5 minutes.

Meanwhile, soak the noodles for 3 minutes in warm water, then drain and rinse under cold water. Drain before dividing the noodles among four bowls.

Add the shrimp, fish sauce, lemon juice, sugar, and mushrooms to the broth and simmer for 2 to 3 minutes until the shrimp turn white. Pour immediately over the noodles and garnish with fresh lime and lime leaf.

1 Tbsp vegetable oil
2 cloves garlic, shredded
2 shallots, shredded
½-in piece fresh ginger, thin sliced
2 to 4 jalapeño or serrano chiles, chopped
6 cups chicken broth
3 kaffir lime leaves, sliced
One 4-in piece lemon grass, chopped
7 oz rice vermicelli
20 large shrimp, shelled and deveined
6 Tbsp fish sauce
6 Tbsp lemon or lime juice
2 Tbsp granulated brown sugar
16 canned straw mushrooms
Shredded lime leaf, to garnish

Serves 4 to 6

Alternative fish: crawfish.

Recommended wine: Vouvray, Chenin Blanc.

Serving suggestion: serve with Vietnamese spring rolls with crab (page 104) and a salad of onions and cucumbers.

crab and sweetcorn soup with chile crab cakes

Here's a meal that pairs two crabmeat classics. The Chinese soup has a creamy, fragrant combination of flavors. The soup is not puréed, and cream corn will ensure it is not too lumpy. If you want to thicken the soup, mix a little cornstarch with some cold broth and add it to the soup just before it's done. The chile crab cakes provide a flavorful counterpoint to the creamy soup. If serrano chiles are not available, substitute jalapeños. The chiles make these crab cakes quite hot. To reduce the heat, remove seeds and veins from the chiles.

Prepare the crab cakes first. Put the crabmeat into a large bowl. If using canned crab, use the liquid from the can too. Using a fork, mix in the remaining ingredients, stirring thoroughly. Store in the refrigerator for a few hours to allow the flavors to blend.

Meanwhile, start to prepare the soup. Bring the corn, crabmeat, broth, seasoning, and soy sauce to a boil in a large pan, stirring to mix the corn and crab evenly throughout the soup. Simmer for 10 minutes.

Form the crab mixture into six small patties. Cook lightly in butter and oil, about 5 to 7 minutes per side.

Just before serving the soup, whisk the egg whites into soft peaks and stir carefully into the soup. Garnish with chopped scallions. Serve the crab cakes with lemon wedges on the side of the crab and sweetcorn soup.

SOUP
One 15-oz can cream corn
8 oz crabmeat, fresh or canned
5 cups well-flavored fish broth
Salt and black pepper
1 Tbsp soy sauce
2 egg whites
4 scallions, chopped

CRAB CAKES
12 oz crabmeat, fresh or canned
2 fresh serrano chiles, seeded and chopped
1½ Tbsp chopped cilantro
¾ cup bread crumbs
1 Tbsp fine chopped onion
1 Tbsp Dijon mustard
1 Tbsp mayonnaise
1½ tsp light soy sauce
¼ tsp pepper
1 tsp butter
1 tsp vegetable oil

Serves 6

Recommended wine: Riesling, Chardonnay.

Serving suggestion: chile crab cakes can be served on their own, with tartare sauce (page 28), and a simple salad of tomatoes and mushrooms in vinaigrette.

grilled seafood soup

The flavors of grilled seafood, smoky grilled tomatoes, and chiles combine to make a deliciously spicy soup. The grilling and broth preparation can be done in advance, and the broth reheated just before eating.

Put the seafood in a nonmetallic bowl or a sealable plastic bag. Mix the olive oil, lime juice, and half the minced garlic together and pour over the seafood, stirring to coat all the pieces.

Refrigerate the seafood while you prepare the barbecue. It will be easier to grill the seafood if it is threaded onto skewers (wooden skewers should be soaked in water for 30 minutes to prevent burning).

Mound coals in the barbecue and allow to burn until the flames have died and the coals are glowing, about 30 minutes. Spread out the coals. Put the seafood, tomato halves cut-side down, and onion slices on the oiled grill or tray. Cook the seafood for 2 to 3 minutes each side. It does not have to be thoroughly cooked since it can finish cooking in the soup, but it should pick up color and flavor from the grilling. Grill the tomatoes until they are soft and have char marks on cut side. Remove from grill, remove skin, and chop. Grill onions until they soften slightly and have char marks, then turn and repeat. Remove from grill. Chop half the onion slices. Separate the other half into rings.

Heat the vegetable oil in a large saucepan. Add the chopped tomatoes, chopped onions, minced garlic, chopped jalapeños, and oregano. Fry for 5 minutes. Add the clam juice or seafood broth and the herbs. Bring to a boil, lower the heat, and simmer, partially covered, for 15 minutes. Remove the lid and add the grilled onion rings, bell pepper, and sliced jalapeño.

Simmer for a further 3 or 4 minutes. Add the seafood and cook for 1 to 2 minutes. Add salt and pepper to taste.

Serves 4

¾ lb shrimp, peeled and deveined
¾ lb scallops
¼ cup olive oil
¼ cup lime juice
5 cloves garlic, minced
3 large tomatoes, cored and halved
1 large yellow onion, peeled and
 thick sliced
1 Tbsp olive or vegetable oil
4 jalapeño chiles, chopped
1 tsp fresh or ¼ tsp dried oregano
5 cups bottled clam juice or fish broth
 (page 26)
1 Tbsp fresh or 1 tsp dried basil
1 tsp fresh or ¼ tsp dried thyme
½ bell pepper, diced
1 or 2 jalapeño chiles, sliced into
 thin rounds
Salt and pepper to taste

Alternative fish: clams, mussels, squid, or a mixture of these.

Recommended wine: young white Bordeaux.

Serving suggestion: serve with wedges of cheese quesadillas.

smoked salmon chowder

Two kinds of salmon make this chowder doubly rich. First, fresh salmon is poached in a vegetable broth, adding a delicate flavor. Later, smoked salmon is added, making this a very filling soup. Fresh dill and chives add the perfect finishing touch.

1 Tbsp butter
3 to 4 shallots, fine chopped
2 sticks celery, fine chopped
5 cups water
1 bay leaf
2 salmon steaks (about 1 lb total weight)
2 potatoes (about 1 lb), diced
1¼ cups light cream
Black pepper
7 oz smoked salmon, cut in small pieces
1 Tbsp chopped dill
1 Tbsp snipped chives

Melt the butter in a heavy pan over medium-low heat. Add the shallots and celery, and sweat until slightly softened. Add the water and bay leaf, cover, and simmer gently for 10 minutes.

Add the salmon steaks and poach for 10 minutes over low heat, covered. Transfer to a plate and allow the fish to cool slightly. Discard the salmon skin and bones, and flake the flesh coarsely.

Meanwhile, stir the potatoes into the cooking liquid and allow to simmer for 15 to 20 minutes, partially covered, until they are tender.

Add the cream to the chowder, season with pepper, and simmer for about 5 minutes to heat through. Stir in the poached salmon, smoked salmon pieces, and herbs, and continue cooking for 5 minutes. Taste for seasoning, and ladle into warm soup plates or bowls.

Serves 6

Alternative fish: trout or grouper.

Recommended wine: Pinot Gris.

Serving suggestion: cold asparagus salad and fresh bread.

san francisco cioppino

If San Francisco has a signature dish, it is cioppino, a wonderful seafood stew that highlights the Pacific Ocean's Dungeness crab. Its origins are in a modest Italian fish soup, which in turn is a more rustic version of *bouillabaisse*. The broth is a rich, garlic-flavored tomato one, which usually includes wine. Be sure to provide tools for cracking crab shells, finger bowls, and plenty of napkins.

In a very large saucepan or stockpot, heat ½ cup olive oil. Add the onion, leeks, and peppers. Sauté for 10 minutes.

Meanwhile, heat the remaining 2 tablespoons olive oil in a very small sauté pan. Add the garlic and sauté for 2 minutes. If the garlic browns too quickly, remove the pan from the heat. The residual heat in the oil will continue to cook the garlic. Add the garlic and oil to the saucepan.

Add the tomatoes, herbs, pepper flakes, wine, and fish broth to the pan. Bring the soup to a boil, then lower the heat and allow to simmer, uncovered, for 45 minutes. Taste, adding more red pepper flakes if a spicier broth is desired, and add salt if needed. If you are making the broth in advance, remove it from the heat, cool, and refrigerate. About 30 minutes before serving, return it to the stove and bring it to a boil.

Add the seafood in this order: first, the crab, about 15 minutes before serving time. Add the mussels or clams about 5 minutes later. Add the fish 7 to 8 minutes before serving time, and finally, about 3 minutes before eating, add the shrimp.

Remove and discard the bay leaves, as well as any mussels or clams whose shells have failed to open. Put some seafood in each bowl, making sure everyone gets a selection, then ladle some broth over it.

½ cup plus 2 Tbsp olive oil
1 large onion, chopped
3 leeks, white part only, chopped
1 red and 1 green bell pepper, chopped
8 cloves garlic, minced
1½ lb fresh tomatoes, peeled, seeded, and chopped, or three 15-oz cans whole tomatoes, chopped
4 Tbsp chopped parsley
2 tsp dried basil
1 tsp dried oregano
½ tsp dried thyme
2 bay leaves
¼ tsp dried red pepper flakes, or more to taste
2 cups dry red wine, such as Pinot Noir
9 cups fish broth, bought or homemade (see method)
Salt to taste
2 large Dungeness crabs, cooked, cracked, and cleaned
2 dozen clams in their shells, scrubbed
2 dozen mussels in their shells, scrubbed
1 lb sea bass, swordfish, or other sturdy, non-oily fish, cut into 1-in cubes
1½ lb shrimp, shelled and deveined

Serves 10 to 12

Alternative fish: golden crab or other fresh local crab, lobster, scallops, or squid.

Recommended wine: Zinfandel, Pinot Noir

Serving suggestion: serve with a simple green salad and sourdough bread.

Many of the recipes in this section feature the most popular and widely available fish in the repertoire of world cuisine – cod, haddock, and snapper. They are extremely versatile fish and can be cooked in a variety of ways, including frying, baking, and steaming and they stand up well to a wide range of sauces, both delicate and robust. Trout, catfish (which is enjoying something of a revival after many years of neglect by cooks), and the mighty salmon, regarded by many as the king of all fish, are traditional favorites which remain as popular as ever. The fish in this section combine with a number of different ingredients to produce powerful flavor combinations, from herbs and citrus fruits to garlic, ginger, and chiles. Pan-fried Salmon with Warm Black-Bean Corn Relish or Baked Trout Stuffed with Tabbouleh illustrate how these fish can be complemented by the addition of powerful accompanying flavors that provide more than a worthy match for their own flavor and texture.

citrus-spiced Pacific cod with red bell pepper caponata and couscous

Serve this Mediterranean-inspired dish with a little red bell pepper caponata, a spicy variation on the traditional Sicilian dish which makes a perfect foil for the fish. The fish is set on a bed of couscous, used widely in Mediterranean cooking.

Combine the fish with the garlic, orange juice, lemon juice, cumin, ginger, turmeric, paprika, salt, cayenne, and half the olive oil. Toss to mix well and allow to marinate for 30 to 60 minutes.

Meanwhile, make the caponata. Lightly sauté the onion, pepper, and sliced garlic in the olive oil until soft. Sprinkle with salt as they cook, then add the tomatoes, jalapeño, cumin, turmeric, ginger, saffron, fennel, and sugar, and continue to cook for about a further 10 minutes, or until thickened and saucelike.

Stir in the capers, olives, seedless raisins, and lemon juice, then taste for seasoning; you want a sweet-sour-spicy balance, so adjust the sugar, lemon juice, and spices accordingly. Stir in the marjoram or parsley and reserved chopped garlic, taste for seasoning, and allow to cool.

Remove the fish from the marinade, pat dry, and lay on a pan. Brush with the remaining oil and cook under a hot broiler or in a medium-hot grill pan, turning carefully once. Allow only about 5 minutes per side, taking care not to overcook.

While the fish is cooking, make the couscous. In a small saucepan, bring 1¼ cups of water to a boil. Add olive oil and salt. Stir in the couscous. Cover, remove from the heat, and allow to stand for 5 minutes.

Spoon couscous onto serving plates, add a piece of fish, and top with the cold red bell pepper caponata.

Serves 4

1¾ lb cod or haddock fillets
4 cloves garlic, peeled and thin sliced
  or chopped
2 Tbsp orange juice
Juice of ½ lemon
¼ tsp cumin
⅛ tsp each ginger, turmeric, paprika
Salt and cayenne to taste
6 to 7 Tbsp extra-virgin olive oil
1½ cups couscous
2 tsp olive oil
½ tsp salt

CAPONATA
1 onion, thin sliced
1 red bell pepper, chopped
4 cloves garlic: three thin sliced and one
  fine chopped
5 to 6 Tbsp extra-virgin olive oil
Salt to taste
4 to 5 ripe tomatoes (canned is fine, use
  the juice as well)
1 jalapeño chile, seeds and veins removed,
  fine chopped
Pinch each cumin, turmeric, dried ginger,
  saffron threads
⅛ tsp fennel seeds or ¼ bulb fennel, diced
2 Tbsp sugar or to taste
1 to 2 Tbsp capers, drained
About 10 green or black Mediterranean
  olives, pitted and halved
2 Tbsp seedless raisins
Juice of 1 lemon or to taste
1 Tbsp chopped marjoram and/or parsley

Alternative fish: haddock, red snapper, pollock, grouper, rockfish, or turbot.

Recommended wine: Pinot Grigio, Sauvignon Blanc.

Serving suggestion: serve with winter squash purée with roasted garlic (page 113).

oven-baked salt cod with olives and potatoes

The salt cod for this dish must be soaked for 24 hours before it is prepared. If you cannot find salt cod, use fresh cod instead, which won't need soaking. Don't forget to remove the skin.

Place the salt cod in a large bowl and cover with cold water. Soak, refrigerated, for 24 hours, changing the water several times. Place the cod in a large pan, breaking it into several chunks to fit. Cover with water. Bring to a boil, then lower the heat and simmer for 5 to 7 minutes. Discard the water and skin the fish, then flake with your fingers, looking out for bones.

Preheat the oven to 425°F. In a large saucepan, heat the olive oil and gently fry the onions, garlic, and parsley until the onions become translucent. Add the salt cod and the sliced potatoes to the saucepan and cook for 10 minutes. Taste, and adjust for seasoning.

Transfer the mixture to a large ovenproof dish. Bake in the oven for 10 to 15 minutes. Decorate with the egg slices and green olives to serve.

3 lb dry salt cod
¼ cup olive oil
4 onions, sliced into fine rings
3 cloves garlic, chopped
2 tsp chopped parsley
14 oz potatoes, boiled and cut into
    1-in slices
Salt and black pepper
3 hard-cooked eggs, sliced

Serves 4 to 6

Alternative fish: fresh cod.

Recommended wine: Pinot Gris.

Serving suggestion: serve with oven-baked tomatoes (page 115) and a green salad.

spanish-style haddock

This traditional Spanish dish is very similar to Mexican dishes where cod or other firm, white-fleshed fish is marinated in lime juice. This is not as highly spiced as a typical Mexican dish would be, and the lightly cooked vegetables add texture and variety.

Cut the fish into bite-size pieces. Heat 2 tablespoons of the oil in a skillet and fry the fish until just done. Transfer it to a glass or china dish. Heat the remaining oil in the skillet; add the onion and garlic and cook until soft but not browned. Stir in the mushrooms and peppers and cook for a further 1 to 2 minutes – the vegetables should retain a crisp texture. Spoon the vegetables over the fish and season lightly.

Pour the vinegar and water into the skillet and bring to a boil. Stir in the sugar until dissolved, then pour the liquid over the fish and vegetables. Allow to cool, then cover and chill in the refrigerator.

1 lb thick haddock fillet or similar white
  fish, skinned
3 Tbsp olive oil
1 mild onion, fine sliced
2 plump cloves garlic, fine sliced
1½ cups sliced button mushrooms
1 red and 1 green bell pepper, seeded
  and sliced
Salt and black pepper
½ cup white wine vinegar
½ cup water

Serves 4

Alternative fish: most mild-flavored, white-fleshed fillets can be substituted, including cod, grouper, red snapper, sea bass, and ocean perch.

Recommended wine: Sauvignon Blanc, dry Gewürztraminer.

Serving suggestion: whole wheat bread and a tomato salad.

red snapper with summer-green sauce

This is a Jewish–Mexican recipe, which involves baking the snapper in a blanket of vegetable and herb purée to keep the flesh moist and tender.

Lightly grease a deep baking pan. Place the fish in the center of the dish and rub with a little lime juice. Sprinkle with salt and pepper to taste. Set aside.

Make the sauce. In a food processor fitted with a metal blade, process the lettuce, cucumber, green bell pepper, red onion, garlic, watercress, scallions, and cilantro with the remaining lime juice. Pour the sauce over the fish, cover, and refrigerate for at least 2 hours.

Preheat the oven to 350°F. Uncover the fish and bake, basting twice, until it is opaque and flesh flakes when pierced with a knife, 20 to 25 minutes. Transfer to a serving platter. Pour over the sauce from the baking pan and garnish with cherry tomatoes, olives, and cilantro.

Vegetable oil, to grease
3 to 4 lb red snapper or sea bass fillets
Juice of 5 limes
Salt and black pepper

SAUCE
1 head Romaine lettuce, trimmed, cored, and shredded
½ cucumber, peeled and seeded
1 small green bell pepper, cored, seeded, and chopped
1 red onion, quartered
3 to 4 cloves garlic
1 small bunch watercress, stems trimmed
4 to 5 scallions, trimmed
3 to 4 Tbsp cilantro
Cherry tomatoes, ripe olives, chopped cilantro, to garnish

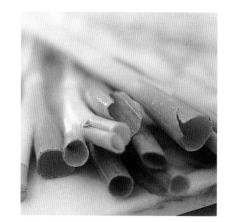

Serves 6

Alternative fish: halibut, sea bass, ocean perch, haddock.

Recommended wine: Voignier, Sauvignon Blanc.

Serving suggestion: roasted potatoes in sweet hot sauce (page 117) and oven-baked tomatoes (page 115).

caribbean red snapper

Red snapper is one of the Caribbean's most delectable fishes and their rich, meaty flesh goes well with strong-flavored sauces. In this dish the mix of spices and tomatoes permeates the fish with wonderful West Indian flavors.

Preheat the oven to 400°F. Coat a 13 x 9 x 2-inch baking pan with vegetable oil. Arrange the sliced onion in the pan and add the tomato, allspice, oregano, thyme, cilantro, and bay leaf. Combine the water and hot pepper sauce and gently pour over the tomato mixture. Rub the fish fillets with lime or lemon juice and arrange carefully in the dish.

Fry the garlic, onion, and bell peppers in olive oil for about 3 minutes. Spoon over the fish. Cover and bake in the oven for 40 to 45 minutes or until the fish flakes easily when tested with a fork. Remove the bay leaf and garnish with the almonds.

Vegetable oil
1 medium onion, sliced
1 large tomato, peeled and chopped
½ tsp allspice
¼ tsp dried oregano
¼ tsp dried thyme
1 tsp chopped cilantro, or to taste
½ bay leaf
2 Tbsp water
1 tsp hot pepper sauce
1 lb red snapper fillets
½ Tbsp lime or lemon juice
1 small clove garlic, minced
½ large onion, chopped
¼ red and ¼ green bell pepper, chopped
½ Tbsp olive oil
3 Tbsp sliced almonds

Serves 4

Alternative fish: perch, turbot, sole, grouper, halibut, or haddock.

Recommended wine: Chianti, Sauvignon Blanc.

Serving suggestion: fried coconut rice (page 120).

baked trout stuffed with tabbouleh

Whole trout bake very successfully in the claypot. This dish of tender fish, bulgur wheat, diced salad vegetables, and the fresh flavors of mint and parsley, is perfect for a light summer lunch or supper. If you do not have a claypot, alternative baking instructions are included.

Presoak the claypot as directed and line the bottom with waxed paper. Wash the trout inside and out, and pat dry using paper towels. Season the cavities with salt and pepper, and set aside.

For the stuffing, mix all the ingredients together, except the yogurt, and reserving some mint and parsley for garnish. Spoon some stuffing into the cavity of each trout and transfer them to the claypot. Any remaining stuffing mixture can be chilled and served as a salad accompaniment. Spoon the white wine over the trout, cover, and place in a cold oven. Set the oven to 425°F and cook for 45 minutes or until the trout are done.

If you are not using a claypot, preheat the oven to 350°F. Place each stuffed trout on a large piece of foil and spoon the wine over the trout. Fold the foil over the trout and seal. Bake for about 25 minutes, or until the trout flakes.

Four trout, 8 oz each, cleaned and heads
  removed
Salt and black pepper
4 Tbsp dry white wine
Lemon wedges, mint, and parsley,
  to garnish

TABBOULEH STUFFING
½ cup bulgur wheat, soaked according to
  the manufacturer's instructions
¼ cup fine diced cucumber
4 medium tomatoes, seeded and fine
  chopped
4 scallions, trimmed and fine chopped
2 Tbsp chopped mint
2 Tbsp chopped parsley
1 Tbsp lemon juice

SAUCE
¾ cup plain yogurt
2 Tbsp chopped mint
2 Tbsp chopped parsley
Salt and pepper

Serves 4

Alternative fish: pompano, red snapper.

Recommended wine: Lugana, Sauvignon Blanc.

Serving suggestion: steamed vegetables, such as carrots or broccoli.

pan-fried salmon with warm black-bean corn relish

This warm, spicy relish with its rich partnership of flavors is the perfect complement to lightly fried salmon. For a milder relish, remove the seeds and veins of the jalapeños or omit them entirely. If the weather is good, salmon is delicious grilled on an outdoor barbecue.

Have all the relish ingredients ready.

Season the salmon on both sides with salt and pepper. Heat the olive oil in a large skillet. Add the salmon and cook over medium heat, turning once, until the fish just starts to flake and just a bit of dark pink flesh can be seen in the center, 3 to 5 minutes each side, depending on the thickness of the steaks.

While the salmon is cooking, heat the corn, black beans, olive oil, and lime juice in a medium saucepan until the corn is done, about 5 minutes. Add the remaining ingredients and cook over medium heat just until warmed through.

Serve the salmon steaks topped with a large spoonful of relish.

4 salmon steaks, about 6 oz each
Salt and pepper
1 Tbsp olive oil

BLACK-BEAN CORN RELISH
1 cup fresh or frozen corn kernels
One 15-oz can black beans
2 Tbsp olive oil
2 Tbsp lime juice
¼ cup diced red bell pepper
¼ cup diced green bell pepper
2 tomatoes, seeded and chopped
¼ cup chopped scallions
2 Tbsp chopped cilantro
1 or 2 jalapeño chiles, minced
¼ tsp ground cumin
¼ tsp salt
Pinch black pepper

Serves 4

Alternative fish: whole trout, swordfish, tuna, monkfish.

Recommended wine: Chardonnay, Chablis; if grilled, Pinot Noir.

Serving suggestion: roasted potatoes in sweet hot sauce (page 117) and roasted portobellos with pine nuts, peppercorns, and chervil (page 117).

taramasalata

Tarama is the salted, dried, lightly smoked roe of gray mullet or cod, usually sold as a paste in jars. In Corfu, however, smoked herring roe, which can be bought whole and mashed into a paste, is preferred. This dense, pinky-orange, pressed-egg mixture is whipped into the classic Greek dish taramasalata, a pink dip or spread enriched with olive oil and flavored with onion and lemon juice.

Soak the bread in cold water for a minute or two, then squeeze it dry.

Place the tarama, soaked bread, potato, garlic, onion, and lemon juice in a blender, and beat until it forms a thick paste. Blend until smooth or slightly textured, as preferred.

Slowly add the olive oil, a few tablespoons at a time, blending in between, until a thick mixture is formed. If the flavor is too strong or heavy and the texture too dense, blend in a few tablespoons of water. Remove from the blender and spoon into a bowl.

Stir in the dill and scallions, and chill. Serve garnished with black olives.

3 slices country bread
½ cup tarama
1 freshly boiled potato, lightly mashed
1 to 2 cloves garlic, minced
1 small or ½ medium onion, chopped
Juice of 2 lemons
¾ to 1 cup extra-virgin olive oil,
    preferably Greek
Several sprigs dill, chopped
2 to 3 scallions, thin sliced
Greek black olives, to garnish

OCEAN AND FRESHWATER ROUNDFISH

Serves 4 to 6

Recommended wine: Brut champagne.

Serving suggestion: serve as an appetizer, with fresh bread and aromatic olives.

Although rather unprepossessing in appearance because of their flat shape, small flatfish such as sole, skate, and flounder are exquisitely delicate in flavor and can be transformed into elegant seafood classics from Sole Meunière to Fish Fillets en Papillote. Larger flatfish such as turbot, which is native to the North Atlantic, and halibut are prized by chefs the world over. Poached in court-bouillon and served whole, with a simple accompaniment of hollandaise or mayonnaise, they make an impressive dish for a celebration meal. Skate, which is round in most waters of the world, is elegant in shape because of its wings and, unusually for seafood, improves if refrigerated for one or two days prior to cooking. Flatfish fillets or steaks can be pan-fried or baked and served simply with lemon wedges or a flavored butter to complement them. Fillets can also be filled with stuffing and rolled up. The recipes in this section provide suggestions for cooking flatfish in both a simple or more elaborate way, from the delicate Skate with Tarragon Butter to the intriguingly flavored Cuban-style Halibut with Rice.

moroccan halibut and pepper brochettes

Charmoula **is a Moroccan sauce of sweet roasted bell peppers, spices, and herbs in which chunks of fish are marinated overnight. The fish is then threaded onto skewers with pieces of bell pepper and barbecued.**

Cut one red bell pepper into three or four nearly flat pieces. Place under a broiler, skin-side up. Cook until the skins are blistered and almost solidly black. Remove from the oven and place in a paper bag for at least 10 minutes. The skin will then peel off easily.

Chop the roasted bell pepper and put it in a food processor with the onion, garlic, paprika, cumin, cayenne, salt, olive oil, and 1 tablespoon each of the parsley and cilantro. Purée to make a thick sauce. Put the halibut in a bowl, add the sauce, and stir so all the pieces are coated. Allow to marinate at least overnight or, ideally, for up to 24 hours.

Cut the three remaining bell peppers into chunks. Thread the fish onto skewers, alternating with pieces of bell pepper.

Light the barbecue. Grill the kabobs over charcoal until lightly browned on each side, 7 to 8 minutes in total.

Serve sprinkled with the remaining parsley and cilantro. Accompany with lemon wedges and hot sauce on the side, for those who enjoy a spicier flavor.

2 red bell peppers, 1 yellow bell pepper,
   1 green bell pepper
1 small onion, cut into chunks
5 garlic cloves, chopped
½ tsp each paprika and cumin
Several pinches cayenne
½ to 1 tsp salt or to taste
6 Tbsp extra-virgin olive oil
2 Tbsp each chopped parsley and cilantro
Juice of 1 lemon
1 lb halibut, cut into bite-size pieces
1 lemon, cut into wedges
Hot pepper sauce

Serves 4

Alternative fish: any sturdy, meaty fish such as tuna, swordfish, or shark.

Recommended wine: Pinot Grigio.

Serving suggestion: Serve with warm lentil and bacon salad (page 121) and a green salad.

fish fillets en papillote

En papillote refers to food cooked in buttered wax paper or foil. Individual waxed paper envelopes are available at many gourmet or specialty kitchen stores, or you can make your own. Serve the fillets with a generous spoonful of butter sauce on the side.

Pick over the crabmeat to ensure there are no bits of shell or cartilage. Lightly oil a large, shallow baking pan. Preheat the oven to 400°F.

Cut the waxed paper into four hearts, each about 12 x 15 inches, but at least 3 inches longer than the fillets. Lightly butter one side of the paper. Fold the hearts in half, with the buttered side on the inside. Place one fillet on the right side of each heart.

Make the topping. In butter in a medium skillet, sauté the mushrooms and scallions for 10 minutes. Sprinkle flour over the mushrooms, stir, and cook for 1 minute. Add cream, salt, and pepper, stir, and cook for 1 minute longer. Remove from the heat. Gently stir in the crabmeat.

Spoon the topping over the four fillets. Fold the left side of each heart over the top. Fold and crimp the edges of the paper so they form enough of a seal to trap the steam from the fish. Place the packages in the baking pan. Bake until the fish flakes easily, about 15 minutes.

Meanwhile, make the sauce.

Combine the onion, wine or champagne, and wine vinegar in a small saucepan. Bring to a boil and cook, stirring frequently and watching closely, until the liquid reduces to 1 tablespoon. Strain the liquid to remove the onion, and return the liquid to the pan. Whisk in the butter, one piece at a time. Then add the cream, tarragon, salt, and pepper, and whisk until smooth.

Serves 4

4 pompano fillets, about 6 oz each
3 Tbsp butter, plus butter for the waxed paper envelopes
2 cups coarse chopped mushrooms
½ cup chopped scallions
1 Tbsp flour
2 Tbsp cream
¼ tsp salt
Pinch pepper
4 oz crabmeat, preferably fresh

BUTTER SAUCE
1 Tbsp fine chopped scallion, white part only
2 Tbsp dry white wine or champagne
2 Tbsp white wine vinegar
6 Tbsp unsalted butter, cut into pieces
2 Tbsp heavy cream
1 tsp fresh chopped or ½ tsp dried tarragon
¼ tsp salt
Pinch white pepper

Alternative fish: turbot, flounder, red snapper.
Recommended wine: Chardonnay.
Serving suggestion: oven-baked tomatoes (page 115) and rice.

This recipe is similar to the Spanish Paella (page 109), but with the addition of sweet spices and dark rum. The dish is cooked in a claypot but an ovenproof glass or ceramic casserole dish may also be used.

Presoak the claypot according to the manufacturer's instructions. In a shallow bowl, mix together the fish, cumin, oregano, cinnamon, lime juice, and seasoning. Cover and chill for at least 30 minutes while you prepare the rice.

Place the onion, garlic, bell peppers, and rice into the claypot and mix well. Pour over the broth and sprinkle in the saffron. Season well. Cover and place in a cold oven. Set the oven to 425°F and cook for 1 hour 15 minutes, stirring occasionally. Stir in the marinated fish and rum, mix well, cover, and cook for a further 30 minutes until the fish is tender and the rice has absorbed any remaining liquid. Check the seasoning and serve straight from the claypot.

If you are not using a claypot, preheat the oven to 350°F. Heat 1 tablespoon vegetable oil in a skillet and add the onion, garlic, and bell peppers. Sauté for 5 minutes then transfer to a 3-quart casserole. Add the rice. Bring the vegetable broth to a boil and add to the rice. Sprinkle saffron over the rice. Cook for 1 hour, stirring occasionally. Stir in the marinated fish and rum, and follow the remaining instructions above. Check the fish for doneness after 20 minutes.

1 lb halibut, cut into 1-in cubes
1 tsp ground cumin
1 tsp dried oregano
1 tsp ground cinnamon
Juice of 1 lime
1 tsp salt
¼ tsp black pepper
1 large onion, peeled and chopped
2 cloves garlic, peeled and minced
1 red, 1 yellow, and 1 green bell pepper, seeded and chopped
1¼ cups long-grain rice, rinsed
5 cups fresh vegetable broth
Large pinch saffron threads
¾ cup dark rum

Serves 4

Alternative fish: firm white fish fillets such as monkfish or cod.

Recommended wine: Pinot Grigio.

Serving suggestion: three types of peas with pesto (page 112).

skate with tarragon butter

Skate is an attractive fish to serve; its meat comes away in long strands and is delicious and tender. This recipe is cooked in a two-tiered steamer. Tarragon and fish are a perfect combination, but dill or fennel tops may be used instead for an equally good sauce.

Rinse the skate under cold water and pat dry with paper towels. Cut the skate wings in half to obtain four equal portions.

Line two steamer tiers with waxed paper and place two portions of fish in each.

Mix the vermouth with half of the orange juice and zest and pour over the fish. Add half of the leek and onion to each tier and stack on top of each other in the steamer base. Cover with a tight-fitting lid and cook for 20 minutes, swapping the tiers over halfway through cooking, until the fish is done.

Meanwhile, melt the butter in a small saucepan and add the remaining orange juice and zest. Stir in the remaining sauce ingredients and heat gently for around 2 to 3 minutes or until thoroughly combined.

Remove the skate from the steamer and transfer to warmed serving plates. Spoon the butter over the skate and garnish with orange slices and tarragon sprigs.

2 medium-size skate wings, about 2 lb
¾ cup dry vermouth
Juice and zest of 1 medium orange
1 small leek, sliced
1 medium red onion, quartered and
   thin sliced

TARRAGON BUTTER
1 stick butter
2 Tbsp chopped tarragon
Few drops tabasco
2 tsp mixed peppercorns, lightly crushed
Salt
Orange slices and tarragon sprigs,
   to garnish

Serves 4

Alternative fish: cod or monkfish.

Recommended wine: Chardonnay.

Serving suggestion: new potatoes and steamed broccoli, drizzled with leftover tarragon butter.

sole meunière on a bed of leeks and spinach

Delicately flavored sole is lightly floured, fried, and topped with a simple parsley-butter sauce. It is served on a bed of leeks and spinach that have been sautéed in butter.

Put the spinach in a large colander and pour boiling water slowly over it. Drain well and allow to cool slightly, then squeeze by hand to remove as much liquid as possible. Heat 1 tablespoon butter in a skillet. Add the leeks and cook over medium-low heat for 5 minutes.

Meanwhile, prepare the sole. Lightly flour the fish and shake off any excess. Melt 4 tablespoons butter in a large skillet (or use 2 skillets). Fry the fillets for about 3 minutes each side. Put the fillets in a warm oven. Add the parsley to the butter in the skillet; add a little extra butter if necessary.

Add 1 tablespoon butter to the leeks, then add the spinach. Sauté for about 2 minutes. Add salt and pepper to taste.

Divide the spinach and leeks among 4 plates. Place a piece of fish on top and drizzle with butter-parsley sauce.

1 lb spinach, stalks removed
¾ stick butter
1 large leek, cut in half lengthwise and thin sliced (white part only)
2 lemon or Dover soles, filleted
½ cup flour
Salt and pepper
1 Tbsp chopped parsley
1 lemon, cut into wedges

Serves 4

Alternative fish: pompano, scallops.

Recommended wine: Vinho verde, Sauvignon Blanc.

Serving suggestion: small red potatoes roasted in olive oil, garlic, and parsley.

pecan-crusted flounder with lime-butter sauce

Aïoli (page 27) can replace the lime-butter sauce as an accompaniment, if preferred.

Season the fillets on both sides with salt and pepper. Whisk the egg, water, and soy sauce together in a large bowl. Dip the fillets, one at a time, in the egg mixture to coat lightly, then dredge evenly in nuts. In a large nonstick skillet over medium-high heat, heat 1 tablespoon of the vegetable oil. When hot, add as many fillets as will fit without crowding. Sauté for about 2 minutes, or until lightly browned on both sides. Add more oil, if needed.

Transfer the fillets to a warm serving plate and wipe the skillet with paper towels. Add the olive oil, remaining vegetable oil, and butter. Heat until the butter foams and starts to brown. Add the lime juice, stir once, then pour the mixture over the fish. Garnish with the herbs and serve.

Salt and pepper to taste
1 large egg
3 Tbsp water
2 tsp dark soy sauce
4 flounder fillets (4–6 oz each), skinned
1 cup pecan nuts, fine chopped
3 Tbsp vegetable oil
2 Tbsp olive oil (optional)
2 Tbsp butter
1 Tbsp freshly squeezed lime juice
3 Tbsp chopped cilantro or parsley, to garnish

Serves 4

Alternative fish: mahi mahi, grouper, sea bass, red snapper.

Recommended wine: Chardonnay, Sauvignon Blanc.

Serving suggestion: roasted sweet potatoes with red pepper-lime butter (page 114) and sautéed spinach with ginger and macadamia nuts (page 120).

Mahi mahi, also known as dolphin fish or dorado, is a frequent catch off the Hawaiian Islands and in other tropical waters. Here it is marinated in lime and ginger, then teamed with another Hawaiian specialty, macadamia nuts. The Ginger-fruit Butter is delicious with broiled or roasted fish. Make it in advance then slice off portions as needed.

To make the Ginger-fruit Butter, mash the softened butter with a fork. Beat in the other ingredients. Roll the mixture into a log and wrap in plastic wrap. Refrigerate until ready to use.

Put the fish in a nonmetallic dish. Combine the lime juice, olive oil, and ginger root and pour over the fish. Allow the fish to marinate for 30 to 60 minutes in the refrigerator, turning the fillets once or twice to ensure they are completely coated in the marinade.

Preheat the oven to 500°F. Lightly oil a cookie sheet or shallow pan large enough to hold all the fillets. While the fish is marinating, grind the nuts in the food processor until they resemble coarse cornmeal. Do not to overgrind or they will turn into nut butter.

Pour the ground nuts into a shallow bowl. Mix the flour, salt, and pepper in another shallow bowl. In a third bowl, beat the egg and milk together with a fork.

Remove the fish from the marinade, and drain, but leave a few bits of ginger clinging to the fish. Dip each fillet in the flour and shake off any excess, dip in the egg-milk mixture, then roll the fillets in nuts until they are evenly coated.

Place the fillets on the cookie sheet or pan. Bake until the fish is opaque but still juicy, 6 to 8 minutes, depending on the thickness of the fillets.

Serves 4

4 mahi mahi fillets, 4 to 6 oz each
⅓ cup lime juice
2 Tbsp olive oil
2 tsp fine grated ginger root
1 cup macadamia nuts
¼ cup flour
Salt and pepper
1 egg
2 Tbsp milk

GINGER-FRUIT BUTTER
1 stick butter, softened
¼ cup puréed mango, papaya, peach, or nectarine
1 Tbsp lime juice
2 tsp grated ginger root
1 tsp snipped chives

Alternative fish: sole, snapper, orange roughy.

Recommended wine: Chardonnay, Sauvignon Blanc.

Serving suggestions: fried coconut rice (page 120) and roasted portobellos with pine nuts, peppercorns, and chervil (page 117).

The boldest, sturdiest fish are found in the depths of the world's oceans. Few fish can match the assertive flavor of tuna, mackerel, swordfish, or monkfish, all of which can tolerate the spiciest of accompanying salsas. Try Lime-marinated Swordfish on Citrus Noodles or Seared Sesame Tuna Salad with Ginger-soy Vinaigrette. Mackerel, rich and oily, works well with a sharp, fruit-based sauce (gooseberry sauce is a classic partner) with enough acidity to counteract the richness. The apple and cucumber salsa featured here is an excellent foil. Fresh tuna, now widely available as steaks, is universally popular and features raw in Japanese sushi. Meaty in texture, these fish work very well in kabobs, brushed with oil then broiled or grilled over hot coals. They also bake very successfully.

seared tuna with cuban mojito sauce

This simple grilled tuna dish is twice-flavored, first with a spicy marinade, then with homemade Cuban Mojito Sauce, an orange-lime-garlic blend that can be used as a marinade for fish and as a pouring sauce after cooking. Grilling over fire is the perfect way to cook tuna, searing the outside and leaving the inside juicy like a good beefsteak.

Combine the tuna with the garlic, salt, cumin, lime juice, black pepper, and cayenne. Leave for about 30 minutes, then remove the fish from the marinade and pat it dry.

Meanwhile, prepare the Mojito Sauce. Place all the ingredients in a jar and shake well until thoroughly blended.

Brush the fish generously with olive oil, then cook quickly either in a skillet or over a barbecue, only about a minute or two each side.

4 tuna steaks, 6 oz each
3 garlic cloves
½ tsp salt
½ tsp cumin
Juice of 2 limes, or juice of 1 orange and 1 lime
Black pepper and cayenne to taste
2 Tbsp extra-virgin olive oil, or as needed

CUBAN MOJITO SAUCE
1 cup orange juice
Juice of 1 lime
½ cup olive oil
3 cloves garlic, minced
2 Tbsp fine chopped bacon
1 Tbsp dry sherry
1 tsp salt
1 tsp dried oregano
½ tsp ground cumin
1 Tbsp grated ginger root

Serves 4

Alternative fish: bluefin and yellowfish tuna, swordfish, salmon, or shark steaks.
Recommended wine: Pinot Noir, Pinot Grigio.
Serving suggestion: fried corn (page 121) and sweet potatoes brushed with olive oil and grilled over the fire.

monkfish and shrimp flambé with orange and garlic

The flavors of orange, garlic, tarragon, bay leaves, and wine create a truly gourmet sauce for this elegant dish. The sauce and fish are flambéed for extra flavor, then the sauce is reduced.

Combine the monkfish and shrimp with the tarragon, bay leaves, garlic, wine, orange juice, orange zest, salt, and pepper. Leave this to marinate for at least an hour, or up to three hours in the refrigerator. Remove the fish and shrimp from their marinade, pat dry and set aside. Reserve the marinade.

Heat a heavy skillet, preferably nonstick, with the olive oil, and when it is very hot, add the shrimp and monkfish, only enough so that they do not crowd the pan. Cook on one side until they just begin to change color, then turn to the other side, and lightly brown them. You want them to stay juicy and not overcook – allow only a few minutes in total. Pour the cognac into the skillet; it will flame up quickly, so be extremely careful and take care of your face, eyebrows, and any curtains near the stove. When the flames die down, remove the shrimp and fish from the skillet.

Add the reserved marinade and reduce down until it forms a flavorful sauce, about five to eight minutes, then return the shrimp, monkfish and juices to the skillet (discarding the bay leaves). Warm through, sprinkle with parsley, and serve.

1½ lb monkfish steaks
8 oz shrimp, peeled and deveined
1 to 2 tsp tarragon leaves
4 to 6 bay leaves, broken in half
10 garlic cloves, chopped
1 cup dry white wine
1 cup orange juice
Grated zest of ½ orange
Salt and pepper to taste
¼ cup extra-virgin olive oil
2 Tbsp cognac
1 Tbsp chopped parsley

Serves 4

Alternative fish: scallops.

Recommended wine: dry Chardonnay.

Serving suggestion: buttered rice and lightly seasoned asparagus.

broiled mackerel with apple and cucumber salsa

Mackerel is a very undervalued fish. It is a rich source of the cholesterol-busting omega-3 oils, and is well partnered by a spicy apple and cucumber salsa. Weather permitting, grill the mackerel on an outdoor barbecue, as it will benefit from the smoky flavors.

Heat a skillet, then add the mustard seeds and fry them for less than 1 minute, until fragrant. Turn into a bowl and add all the ingredients for the salsa. Leave for 20 to 30 minutes, to allow the flavors to blend.

Preheat the broiler. Cover the rack with lightly oiled foil to make cooking and cleaning up easier. Lightly season the mackerel fillets, then broil skin-side up for 3 to 4 minutes, depending on size. Turn the fillets carefully and broil for a further 3 to 4 minutes, until almost done.

Scatter the oatmeal over the fish to form a light topping and cook for a further 1 to 2 minutes, until lightly browned.

Serve the cooked mackerel with plenty of salsa.

SALSA
1 Tbsp white mustard seeds
2 red apples, cored and diced
½ medium cucumber, diced
Grated zest and juice of 1 lemon
1 carrot, diced
1 hot red chile, seeded and fine chopped
2 tomatoes, seeded and diced
1 Tbsp white wine vinegar
Salt and black pepper

8 mackerel fillets
1 Tbsp medium oatmeal

Serves 4

Alternative fish: salmon, tuna.

Recommended wine: Voignier, Chardonnay.

Serving suggestion: winter squash purée with roasted garlic (page 113) and roasted portobellos with pine nuts, peppercorns, and chervil (page 117).

sea bass with asian vegetables

When mature, a whole sea bass extends to nearly a yard in length. It is a fine-flaked white fish, free of small bones. Firm steaks work best in this recipe because they hold their shape well during baking. If you do not have a claypot for this recipe, alternative cooking instructions are included below.

Presoak the claypot according to the manufacturer's instructions. Place all the vegetables inside, together with the ginger and garlic cloves, and mix well.

Wash and pat dry the sea bass steaks using paper towels. Rub the flesh side with the five-spice powder and arrange the steaks on the top of the vegetables. Mix the soy sauce and rice wine or sherry together and spoon over the fish and vegetables.

Cover and place in a cold oven. Set the oven to 425°F and cook for 35 to 40 minutes until the fish is done. Serve each fish steak on a bed of the vegetables and garnish with shredded leeks and snipped chives.

If you are not using a claypot, preheat the oven to 350°F. Heat 1 tablespoon vegetable oil in a skillet. Add the vegetables, ginger, and garlic and sauté for 5 minutes. Transfer the vegetable mixture to a large casserole dish with a lid. If there are not a lot of natural juices in the vegetable mixture, add 1 to 2 tablespoons of liquid to the vegetables – water, white wine, clam juice, or even chicken broth. Prepare the sea bass as directed above, place on top of vegetables, and add the soy sauce and rice wine or sherry. Cover and bake until the fish flakes, about 25 minutes.

2 large carrots, peeled and cut into matchsticks
1 red and 1 yellow bell pepper, seeded and fine sliced
4 oz snow peas, trimmed and fine shredded
1 large zucchini, trimmed and cut into matchsticks
1 large leek, trimmed and shredded
One 1-in piece ginger root, peeled and fine shredded
2 cloves garlic, peeled and minced
Four sea bass steaks, about 6 oz each
2 tsp Chinese five-spice powder
2 Tbsp dark soy sauce
2 Tbsp rice wine or sweet sherry
Deep fried leek and snipped chives, to garnish

Serves 4

Alternative fish: croaker, red snapper, porgy, tilefish.

Recommended wine: Sauvignon Blanc, Riesling.

Serving suggestion: buttered noodles or fried coconut rice (page 120).

lime-marinated swordfish on citrus noodles

Swordfish readily absorbs the flavors of marinades and lime gives it a particularly fresh flavor. In this dish the swordfish is served over noodles seasoned with a citrus-flavored butter. The fish is equally delicious grilled over hot coals.

Mix all the ingredients for the marinade in a shallow dish, then add the swordfish. Marinate in the refrigerator for 2 to 4 hours, turning several times and spooning the marinade over the fish.

Bring salted water to a boil in a large pot. Time the cooking of the noodles so they are done at about the same time as the fish. Add the noodles to the boiling water and cook. Drain.

While noodles are cooking, combine the melted butter, orange juice, lime zest, nutmeg, and salt and pepper and mix well.

Heat the oil in a large skillet. Drain the swordfish and discard the marinade. Fry the fish quickly in the hot oil, 2 to 3 minutes each side.

Toss the citrus butter with the noodles and divide among four plates. Lay the swordfish steaks on top and serve immediately.

4 swordfish steaks, about ½ inch thick,
about 5 oz each
3 Tbsp olive oil

MARINADE
Grated zest and juice of 2 limes
3 Tbsp olive oil
3 scallions, fine chopped
Salt and black pepper
1 clove garlic, minced
1 Tbsp chopped fresh parsley

NOODLES
12 oz dry noodles, such as linguine or
fettucine
2 Tbsp butter, melted
1 Tbsp orange juice
1 tsp grated lime zest
Pinch grated nutmeg
Salt and pepper to taste

Serves 4

Alternative fish: salmon, tuna, shark, monkfish.

Recommended wine: Sauvignon Blanc.

Serving suggestion: spicy grilled vegetables (page 118).

roasted monkfish wrapped in prosciutto

The Italian flavors in this dish combine very well with the firm, meaty texture of monkfish and its delicate, sweet taste. Serve the fish in slices with tagliatelle, chopped tomatoes, olives, and basil. If you do not have a claypot, alternative cooking instructions are included below.

If using a claypot, presoak it according to the manufacturer's instructions and line the base with waxed paper. Season the fillets with salt and pepper.

Mix half the chopped basil and all of the sun-dried tomatoes, artichokes, garlic, and Parmesan cheese. Spread the mixture over the flatter side of one of the fillets. Place the other fillet on top. Wrap the prosciutto around the fish, overlapping to cover. Transfer to the claypot, if using, cover, and place in a cold oven. Set the oven to 425°F and cook for 45 to 50 minutes until the fish is done.

If you are not using a claypot, preheat the oven to 375°F. Stuff and wrap the fish as directed and set it in the center of a large sheet of heavy-duty aluminum foil. Pour about 2 tablespoons of liquid, such as white wine or clam juice, over the fish, then wrap securely. Bake until the fish flakes, about 25 to 30 minutes.

While the fish is roasting, bring a large pot of salted water to a boil. Time the cooking of the pasta so it finishes cooking at the same time as the fish. Add the pasta to the boiling water, cook, and drain.

Just before the end of the cooking time, gently heat the chopped plum tomatoes in a small saucepan. Stir in the olives and basil and season with just a dash of salt (the olives are already salty) and some black pepper. Toss the cooked pasta in about half the tomato-olive mixture and divide among six plates.

Slice the fish and carefully place over the noodles. Top with some of the remaining tomato-olive mixture.

Serves 6

2 monkfish fillets, 12 oz each
Salt and black pepper
⅓ cup chopped basil
2 sun-dried tomatoes, soaked and fine chopped
6 canned artichoke hearts, drained and chopped
1 clove garlic, minced
2 Tbsp freshly grated Parmesan cheese
6 thin slices prosciutto (Parma ham)
8 plum tomatoes, skinned, seeded, and chopped
⅓ cup chopped black olives
16 oz dry noodles, such as tagliatelle

Alternative fish: grouper, striped bass.

Recommended wine: Chardonnay, light Pinot Noir.

Serving suggestion: three types of peas with pesto (page 112).

This salad dish features tuna marinated in a ginger-soy vinaigrette and dredged with sesame seeds. It is cooked rare to medium-rare, still red in the middle, so be sure to buy only very fresh, high-quality tuna, preferably bluefin or yellowfin tuna. Black sesame seeds are available in Asian markets and gourmet shops.

Make the vinaigrette by puréeing all the ingredients in a blender or food processor.

Place the tuna steaks in a plastic food storage bag. Pour about ⅓ cup of the vinaigrette over the tuna steaks, seal the bag, and shake to coat the fish evenly with the vinaigrette. Refrigerate for 1 to 4 hours. Set the remaining vinaigrette aside for use later on.

Heat a cast-iron skillet over medium heat. Add the peanut oil. Remove the tuna steaks from the marinade and dredge on both sides with sesame seeds. Discard the marinade. Sear the steaks until brown on both sides, about 3 minutes each side. The fish should still have a streak of red in the center when cut open.

Divide the greens among six serving plates. Reserve ¼ cup of the vinaigrette and toss the greens in the remaining dressing.

Slice each tuna steak thinly on the diagonal; spread out the pieces from each steak into a fan shape and place over the greens on each plate. Drizzle the reserved vinaigrette over the tuna and serve.

Serves 4

GINGER-SOY VINAIGRETTE
1 small onion, peeled and quartered
One 2-in piece ginger root, peeled
    and diced
⅓ cup cilantro
2 cloves garlic, peeled
⅓ cup soy sauce
3 Tbsp rice wine vinegar
½ cup vegetable oil
2 tsp sesame oil

4 tuna steaks, 1 inch thick,
    about 6 oz each
1 Tbsp peanut oil
¼ cup black sesame seeds
¼ cup white sesame seeds
6 cups mixed salad greens

Alternative fish: swordfish, halibut.

Recommended wine: Sauternes.

Serving suggestion: Asian egg noodles, angel hair pasta, or other thin egg noodles tossed in the ginger-soy vinaigrette.

DEEP SEA FISH

salade niçoise with tarragon vinaigrette

This famous salad from France makes a wonderful, refreshing lunch or dinner on a warm day.

Thoroughly combine all the ingredients for the tarragon vinaigrette in a blender or food processor.

Wash and dry the lettuce, tear into small pieces, and put in a salad bowl. Sprinkle a few tablespoons of the vinaigrette over the top. Arrange the beans, potatoes, and tuna on top of the salad greens, and place the tomatoes around the edge of the bowl. Top with the eggs and anchovies. Pour over the remaining vinaigrette, sprinkle with fresh tarragon, chervil, or parsley, and serve.

1 head Boston lettuce
2 cups cooked green beans
2 cups diced cooked potatoes
1 cup drained and flaked canned tuna
2 to 3 tomatoes, peeled and quartered
2 hard-cooked eggs, quartered
6 anchovies, cut in half
1 Tbsp chopped tarragon, chervil,
   or parsley

TARRAGON VINAIGRETTE
1 egg yolk
2 Tbsp white wine vinegar
1 Tbsp fresh lemon juice
⅔ cup olive oil
Pinch pepper
Pinch salt, if desired
2 Tbsp fresh or 2 tsp dried tarragon

Serves 4 to 6

Alternative fish: broiled mackerel, mahi mahi, salmon, or shrimp.

Recommended wine: Sauvignon Blanc.

Serving suggestion: crusty bread or breadsticks.

smoked fish pâté

This pâté makes a flavorful appetizer.

Coarsely chop the fish and place in a mixing bowl. Add the relish, horseradish, onion, celery, and lime juice and mix well. Add half the hot pepper sauce and half the mayonnaise. Blend together and taste. Add more hot pepper sauce, if necessary, according to taste. Blend in more mayonnaise and mix until the desired texture and flavor are achieved.

1 lb smoked grouper
4 oz sweet pickle relish
¼ cup prepared horseradish sauce
1 small onion, chopped
1 stick celery, peeled and fine chopped
½ tsp lime juice
1 tsp hot pepper sauce
6 Tbsp mayonnaise
Salt and black pepper

Serves 6 to 8

Alternative fish: any smoked fish including trout, kingfish, and marlin.

Recommended wine: Sauvignon Blanc.

Serving suggestion: fresh bread or crackers.

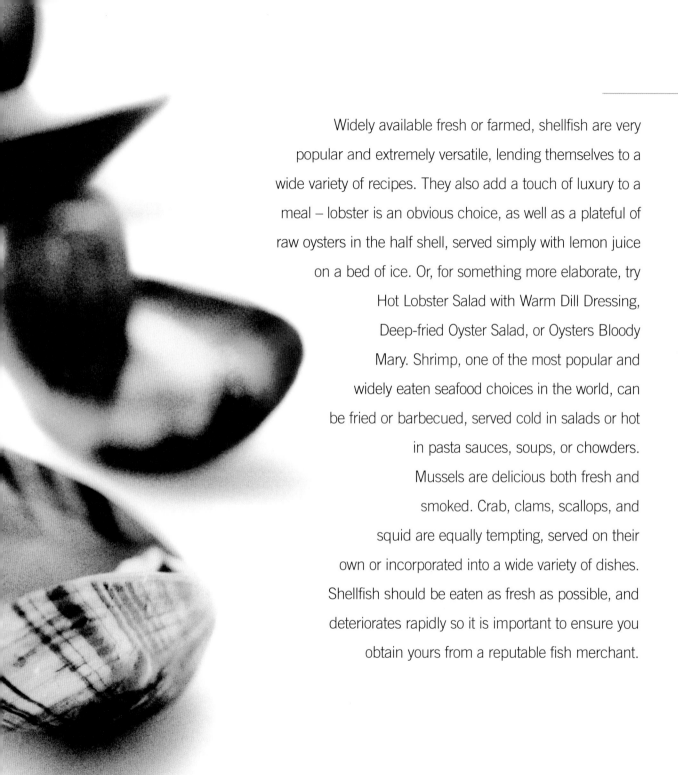

Widely available fresh or farmed, shellfish are very popular and extremely versatile, lending themselves to a wide variety of recipes. They also add a touch of luxury to a meal – lobster is an obvious choice, as well as a plateful of raw oysters in the half shell, served simply with lemon juice on a bed of ice. Or, for something more elaborate, try Hot Lobster Salad with Warm Dill Dressing, Deep-fried Oyster Salad, or Oysters Bloody Mary. Shrimp, one of the most popular and widely eaten seafood choices in the world, can be fried or barbecued, served cold in salads or hot in pasta sauces, soups, or chowders. Mussels are delicious both fresh and smoked. Crab, clams, scallops, and squid are equally tempting, served on their own or incorporated into a wide variety of dishes. Shellfish should be eaten as fresh as possible, and deteriorates rapidly so it is important to ensure you obtain yours from a reputable fish merchant.

hot lobster salad with warm dill dressing

Choosing lobster is an acquired skill. The males have larger claws, but the females are believed to have a sweeter flesh. Prices are generally most reasonable in the summer months.

Cut the lobsters lengthwise in half through the shell and remove the meat. Cut into 1-in cubes. Lay a sheet of dampened waxed paper in the base of the steamer top and arrange the lobster and vegetables inside. Cover with a tight-fitting lid and steam over boiling water for 10 minutes until the vegetables are tender and the lobster is hot.

Meanwhile, arrange the salad greens in a shallow serving bowl. Mix the dressing ingredients in a small saucepan and heat gently until hot.

Spoon the lobster and vegetables onto the salad leaves and pour the dressing over the top. Garnish with a sprig of dill and lime wedges and serve immediately.

Two 1-lb cooked lobsters
2 celery sticks, cut into matchsticks
1 medium red onion, halved and shredded
4 cobs baby corn, halved lengthwise
1 medium carrot, cut into matchsticks
¼ cup snow peas, sliced
Mixed salad greens
Dill and lime wedges, to garnish

DILL DRESSING
2 Tbsp olive oil
1 Tbsp lime juice
1 Tbsp white wine vinegar
1 tsp Dijon mustard
2 garlic cloves, peeled and minced
1 Tbsp chopped dill

Serves 4

Alternative fish: cooked shrimp.

Recommended wine: Chardonnay.

Serving suggestion: cheese or warm garlic bread.

deep-fried oyster salad

Deep-fried oysters are served on a salad of mixed greens with Vidalia sweet onions, peaches, and Asiago cheese. The salad greens include bitter greens such as mustard or dandelion mixed in for a flavor contrast.

Combine all the ingredients for the dressing and blend thoroughly. Clean the greens, and tear them into bite-size pieces. Separate the onion slices into rings. Peel the peaches and cut them into chunks. Divide the greens, onions, and peaches among four plates. Toss with the dressing until well-coated. Put four deep-fried oysters on each salad. Sprinkle with Asiago cheese.

To make the fried oysters combine the cornmeal, cornstarch, and seasonings. Dip the oysters in the cornmeal mixture. In a deep skillet or wok, heat oil to 365°F. With tongs, drop in several oysters at a time, but don't crowd them; they should not touch during cooking.

Cook until golden brown, turning once, about 3 minutes. Drain thoroughly on paper towels. Make sure the oil has returned to 365°F before you cook the next batch. Keep the oysters warm in the oven while you fry the remaining oysters.

1 bunch spinach, arugula, or Bibb lettuce
1 bunch dandelion or mustard greens,
   or two heads endive
Several thick slices Vidalia or other
   sweet onion
1 large or 2 small ripe peaches
Asiago cheese
16 fried oysters (see recipe)

DEEP-FRIED OYSTERS
16 medium to large fresh oysters, shucked
⅔ cup cornmeal
⅓ cup cornstarch
½ tsp salt
¼ tsp black pepper
¼ tsp cayenne
Vegetable oil

DRESSING
⅓ cup olive oil
2 Tbsp lemon juice
½ tsp Dijon mustard
1 clove garlic, minced
2 tsp chopped parsley
¼ tsp salt
Pinch black pepper

Serves 4

Recommended wine: Sauvignon Blanc, Chablis.
Serving suggestion: light dinner rolls and cream of tomato or squash soup.

scallops with lime and crab

Marinated in lime, orange juice, ginger, and cognac and topped with crabmeat, these scallops make an elegant *hors d'oeuvre*. The scallops are "cooked" only by the acid in the citrus juices, so buy very fresh, high-quality scallops. These are very handsome served in their shells. If your seafood market does not sell scallops in the shell, you can buy the shells separately at some seafood and kitchen stores.

12 small to medium scallops or 6 large
   scallops (slice the latter across
   horizontally)
Juice of 4 limes
Juice of 2 oranges
1½ Tbsp cognac
1 small piece ginger root, fine chopped
Salt and black pepper
White crabmeat, to garnish

To pry open the scallops place them dark-side of the shell down and slip a sharp knife through the hinge to sever the muscle which holds the scallop to the shell.

Extract the muscle. Wash the scallops thoroughly and place in the refrigerator, in the cleaned shells, on a tray.

Mix the lime juice, orange juice, cognac, ginger, and seasoning together and spoon over the scallops. Marinate for 4 to 6 hours. The scallops will go opaque and be firm to the touch when ready.

Lightly season the crabmeat and flake over the scallops.

Serve well-chilled.

Serves 2 to 3

Recommended wine: Pinot Grigio, Sauvignon Blanc
Serving suggestion: green salad.

This salad celebrates the food of the Pacific Northwest with mussels from the ocean, sweet onions from Washington, hazelnuts from the orchards, and spinach from the cool valleys. The mussels should be prepared early in the day. If you clean the spinach and toast the hazelnuts at the same time, the salad can be assembled at the last minute.

Scrub the mussels with a brush to remove grit. Remove beards. Discard any mussels that do not close when tapped sharply. Put the mussels in a pot. Add wine and 1 cup water. Bring to a boil, cover, and lower the heat. Cook for 5 to 7 minutes until the mussels open. Discard any that fail to open. Put the mussels in a shallow, nonmetallic dish.

While the mussels are cooking, make the vinaigrette. Combine the red wine vinegar, garlic, mustard, olive oil, salt, pepper, and parsley. Whisk or shake until well-blended. Pour over the hot mussels. Cover and refrigerate the mussels for at least 6 hours, occasionally spooning the marinade over mussels.

About 30 minutes before serving time, remove the mussels from the refrigerator and allow them to come to room temperature. Divide the spinach among four plates. Top with onion rings and hazelnuts. Divide the mussels among the plates. Spoon the vinaigrette marinade over the salads.

20 to 24 small mussels
1 cup dry white wine
⅓ cup red wine vinegar
1 clove garlic, minced
2 tsp Dijon mustard
⅔ cup olive oil
¼ tsp salt
⅛ tsp pepper
2 Tbsp chopped parsley
½ lb young spinach leaves, trimmed, washed, dried, and torn into bite-size pieces
4 slices sweet onion, separated into rings
⅓ cup toasted hazelnuts, chopped

Serves 4

Alternative fish: clams

Recommended wine: Sauvignon Blanc.

Serving suggestion: crusty bread and tomato soup with basil.

SHELLFISH

wok-braised squid with vegetables

Many people are discouraged from eating squid by the rubbery texture that is almost synonymous with battered, deep-fried squid rings. When braised, squid has a meltingly tender texture, and lends itself especially well to Chinese cooking. Baby squid is often more tender than the larger version.

Heat the oil in a wok. Add the garlic and ginger and sauté for 1 minute, pressing with the back of a spoon to squeeze out the juices, then remove with a slotted spoon. Add the squid and fry quickly for 1 to 2 minutes until it becomes opaque.

Remove from the wok with a slotted spoon and keep warm. Add the daikon to the wok and cook until lightly browned, adding a little extra oil if necessary, then add the remaining vegetables.

Blend the cornstarch with a little of the water, then add to the wok with the remaining water, sherry, and soy sauce. Bring to a boil, stirring all the time, then return the squid to the wok and mix with the vegetables.

Add the hot pepper sauce. Cover and simmer gently for approximately 15 minutes. Serve immediately.

3 Tbsp vegetable oil
1 clove garlic, minced
1 tsp ginger root, minced
1 lb prepared squid, defrosted if frozen,
   cut into rings and tentacles chopped
1 daikon radish, sliced
1 large green and 1 large red bell pepper,
   cored, seeded, and cut into large pieces
1 large onion, sliced and separated
   into rings
1 stick celery, thin sliced
½ cup water chestnuts
2 Tbsp cornstarch
1 cup water
½ cup sherry
½ cup soy sauce
¼ tsp hot pepper sauce

Serves 3 to 4

Alternative fish: shrimp.

Recommended wine: Sauvignon Blanc, dry Riesling.

Serving suggestion: plain boiled rice or noodles.

feta shrimp with fusilli

Feta cheese and Greek olives give this dish a Mediterranean flavor. It is very quick to prepare so have all your ingredients ready before you start cooking. Time the pasta so it finishes cooking just before the shrimp.

Cook the pasta in plenty of boiling water to which you've added a pinch of salt and a splash of olive oil.

While the pasta is cooking, make the sauce. Heat the olive oil in a large skillet. Add the garlic and sauté for 1 minute, then add the butter, basil, and thyme, and cook for a further minute.

Add to the pan the chopped tomatoes and cook for 2 minutes. Next add the shrimp and sauté until it barely turns pink and is not quite cooked through, about 1 to 2 minutes. Add the wine and pepper, and cook for 1 minute. Lastly blend in the feta cheese and olives.

Remove from the heat. Ladle over the pasta and sprinkle with chives to serve.

1 lb fusilli or other pasta
2 Tbsp olive oil
2 cloves garlic, minced
1 Tbsp butter
1 Tbsp chopped fresh or 1 tsp dried basil
½ tsp fresh or ¼ tsp dried thyme
2 cups chopped tomatoes
1 lb shrimp, shelled and deveined
¼ cup dry white wine
¼ tsp pepper
6 oz feta cheese, crumbled
16 Greek olives
2 tsp snipped chives, to garnish

Serves 4

Alternative fish: crawfish or cooked lobster.

Recommended wine: Chablis, Sémillon/Sauvignon Blanc blend.

Serving suggestion: crusty bread and tossed green salad or a salad of cold asparagus and mushrooms in vinaigrette.

gingered crab and mushroom with vanilla pasta

An unusual and delicious dish, inspired by one served at the Capital Hotel in London's Knightsbridge, this features ginger-scented crab and mushrooms served over homemade noodles seasoned with vanilla.

Grate the larger piece of ginger, including the skin, with a coarse grater. Place the crabmeat in a bowl. Gather up the shreds of ginger in your hand and squeeze their juice over the crab. Leave the crab to marinate in the ginger juice.

Prepare the pasta. Put the flour in a bowl and make a well in the center. Beat the eggs with the vanilla extract and seeds, then pour in the flour. Bind to a stiff dough, then knead thoroughly. Roll out very thinly, or pass the dough through a pasta machine until thin enough to cut into spaghetti. Drape over a pole or the back of a chair to dry until ready to cook.

Bring a large pan of salted water to a boil. Meanwhile, heat the oil in a skillet. Add the mushrooms and chopped ginger and cook gently until soft and lightly browned. Add the pasta to the boiling water and cook for 1 to 2 minutes. Drain and shake dry.

Add the marinated crabmeat and juice to the mushrooms and heat for about 1 minute. Add the pasta and toss the mixture together. Add the chopped tomato and season just before serving.

One 2-in piece ginger root
1½ cups coarse shredded crabmeat
2 cups semolina or all-purpose flour
2 large eggs
Few drops natural vanilla extract
1 vanilla bean, split and seeds removed
⅓ cup light olive oil
2 cups sliced mushrooms
One 1-in piece ginger root, peeled and fine chopped
1 tomato, skinned, seeded, and chopped
Salt and black pepper

Serves 4

Alternative fish: lobster.

Recommended wine: Sauvignon Blanc, dry Riesling.

Serving suggestion: green salad.

vietnamese spring rolls with crab

It is important to use ingredients that will not break through the delicate rice paper – the ingredients must be ground or finely shredded. Wood ear fungus, a type of mushroom; fish sauce, bean thread vermicelli noodles and rice paper can be found at Asian markets. If wood ear fungus is not available, substitute dried mushrooms.

Combine the dipping sauce ingredients and stir well.

Soak the noodles in boiled water until soft. Drain thoroughly, then cut into shorter strands with kitchen scissors. Soak the mushrooms and wood ear fungus in hot, previously boiled water, until soft. Drain and pat dry, then chop.

Place the noodles, mushrooms, wood ear fungus, water chestnuts, garlic, carrot, onion, cilantro, scallions, fish sauce, black pepper, egg, and crabmeat in a large mixing bowl. Knead the mixture by hand until it is stiff enough to be shaped.

Pour boiled water, slightly cooled, into a large bowl. Spread a clean dish towel on your work surface. Dip a rice paper into the water, and place it on the dish towel. The rice paper will become soft and pliable.

Place a small amount of the noodle mixture in the middle of the rice paper, and form into a sausage shape. Fold the bottom edge over the mixture, tucking it under the mixture. Fold the left and right edges over to the middle. Roll the parcel away from you to seal in the mixture. Repeat until all the mixture is used.

Place the spring rolls in a steamer over a pan of boiling water and allow to steam for 3 to 5 minutes. Serve immediately.

To eat, fold a lettuce leaf around the roll and dip into the sauce.

Makes 8 rolls

DIPPING SAUCE
⅔ cup fish sauce
1 clove garlic, fine chopped
1 jalapeño or serrano chile, fine chopped
2 tsp lemon or lime juice
1 tsp cider vinegar
1 tsp granulated sugar
½ cup fine chopped salted peanuts (optional)

SPRING ROLLS
2 oz bean thread vermicelli noodles
12 dried shiitake mushrooms
3 dried wood ear fungus
One 7-oz can water chestnuts, drained and chopped
2 cloves garlic, minced
1 carrot, shredded
1 onion, shredded
2 Tbsp chopped cilantro
2 scallions, sliced
1 Tbsp fish sauce
Black pepper
1 egg, beaten
¼ lb fresh or canned crabmeat, well shredded
8 sheets round *banh trang* rice paper, measuring 8 in across
Vegetable oil, to fry

Alternative fish: shrimp.
Recommended wine: Gewürztraminer, Chenin Blanc.
Serving suggestion: salad of Boston lettuce with mint, cilantro, and cucumber sticks and dipping sauce.

shrimp chow mein with egg noodles

This is simple and delicious. Use fresh shrimp and add them with the bean sprouts. Thread egg noodles are available in Asian markets and some well-stocked supermarkets in Asian neighborhoods, but any kind of noodle can be substituted and cooked according to the directions on the package. This dish makes a complete meal in itself.

Soak the noodles in boiling water until needed, stirring them occasionally to separate the strands. Cook the onion in the oil in a large pan until softened but not browned. Stir in the five-spice powder and cook for a further 1 minute.

Add the zucchini, carrots, pepper, chile, and garlic, then stir-fry for 3 to 4 minutes. Drain the noodles, then add them to the pan with the shrimp and bean sprouts. Mix the sherry, soy sauce, and water together, then pour the mixture into the pan. Cook for 2 to 3 minutes, tossing the vegetables and noodles together in the sauce. Serve piping hot, with extra soy sauce on the side.

3 sheets (8 oz) thread egg noodles
1 large onion, chopped
2 Tbsp sunflower or peanut oil
1 tsp Chinese five-spice powder
1 large zucchini, cut into matchsticks
1 medium carrot, cut into matchsticks
1 green bell pepper, seeded and shredded
1 jalapeño or serrano chile, seeded and
   fine chopped (optional)
2 plump cloves garlic, fine sliced
7 oz peeled shrimp
2 large handfuls bean sprouts
¼ cup sherry
¼ cup soy sauce
½ cup water

Serves 4

Alternative fish: firm white fish – haddock or squid.

Recommended wine: Riesling.

Serving suggestion: prawn crackers, Vietnamese spring rolls with crab (page 104) and dipping sauce.

oysters bloody mary

Serve the oysters on the half shell, topped with this intensely flavorful vodka-based topping.

Mix a traditional Bloody Mary using the tomato juice, vodka, tabasco, Worcestershire sauce, lemon juice, salt, and pepper; mix in a blender with some ice cubes so that it is well-chilled.

Open the oysters carefully (see page 17), and top with the Bloody Mary mix.

Sprinkle over the diced cucumber and celery and serve with lemon wedges.

1½ cups tomato juice
3 Tbsp vodka
5 drops tabasco
1 tsp Worcestershire sauce
1 Tbsp lemon juice
Salt and black pepper
12 fresh oysters
1 small cucumber, diced
1 small stick celery, diced
Lemon wedges to serve

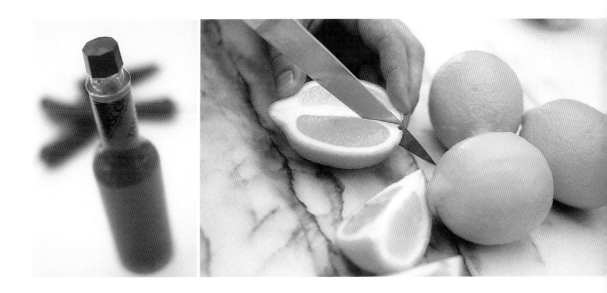

Serving suggestion: thin sliced rye or pumpernickel bread with butter.

spanish paella

Paella is a Spanish peasant dish that originated in Valencia, Spain's rice-growing region, which is why the only true requirement of any traditional paella is that it should contain rice. Most paellas are seasoned with saffron and contain either seafood or meat. The name comes from *paellera*, the large pan in which paella is cooked. Other shellfish can be substituted, and some people like to add chicken or chorizo sausage.

Poach the fish in 2½ cups court-bouillon, for 5 minutes.

Put the oil in a large pan and sweat the garlic, the sliced onion, and half the chopped onion, for about 4 minutes without browning. Add the rice to the pan and stir over the heat for a few minutes until the rice just begins to color.

Strain the fish and reserve the court-bouillon. Add saffron or turmeric to the court-bouillon and pour over the rice, stirring from time to time over low heat. Cook, covered with a lid or foil, for the first 10 minutes.

Blanch the peppers for 2 minutes then dice, add to the rice, and stir well.

In another saucepan, place the chopped onion in the water and wine mixture and season generously. Bring to a boil and add the cleaned mussels. Cook for 10 minutes until steamed open. Discard any that fail to open.

Add the strained mussel liquor to the rice and stir well. Cook for a further 5 minutes or until tender. Add chunks of white fish, shrimp, and mussels.

Serve piping hot sprinkled with parsley and garnished with lemon wedges.

1 lb cod or halibut
2½ cups court-bouillon (page 26)
4 Tbsp oil
2 cloves garlic, minced
1 medium onion, thin sliced and 2 medium onions, fine chopped
1¾ cups long-grain rice
Pinch saffron or turmeric
2½ cups fish broth (page 26) or bottled clam juice
1 red and 1 green bell pepper, seeded
½ cup white wine and ½ cup water, mixed
16 to 20 mussels, bearded and scrubbed
1 cup shelled shrimp
1 Tbsp chopped parsley, to garnish
Lemon wedges, to garnish

Serves 4

Alternative fish: clams, lobster, squid, or a mixture.
Recommended wine: Chablis.
Serving suggestion: serve with a simple tomato salad and fresh bread.

It is important to serve seafood with the appropriate accompaniment, which will enhance it. This section provides a selection of side dishes suitable for serving with the fish and shellfish recipes featured in the book. From Fried Coconut Rice, which works well with many of the Asian-flavored dishes, to Winter Squash Purée with Roasted Garlic, they will add color, texture, and flavor to the seafood and complement it without detracting from its central role.

three types of peas with pesto

The flavor of this selection of peas is enhanced by the basil. To contrast color and texture add a handful of miniature, yellow, summer squashes, cut in half.

8 oz sugar snap peas
8 oz snow peas
1 cup frozen peas

1 Tbsp extra-virgin olive oil
1 clove garlic, chopped
3 Tbsp pesto

Steam the peas, separately, until each is just crisp-tender. The sugar snap peas should take about 2 to 4 minutes, the snow peas about 1 to 3 minutes, and the frozen peas slightly longer.

Rinse the sugar snap peas, snow peas, and cooked frozen peas in cold water to keep them bright green and slightly crunchy. Toss the three types of peas together with the extra-virgin olive oil, chopped garlic, and pesto, and serve at room temperature.

To make your own pesto, process 1 tablespoon of pine nuts, ¼ cup fresh basil leaves, ¼ cup Parmesan cheese, 2 tablespoons olive oil, and a pinch of salt and pepper in a food processor.

Serves 4

**This is a simple dish that provides a lovely contrast
to complex or heavily sauced fish recipes.**

2 medium butternut or acorn squash (about 3 lb in total)	3 Tbsp butter
4 cloves garlic	¾ cup milk
2 to 3 Tbsp olive oil	½ tsp dried thyme
	Salt and pepper

Preheat the oven to 400°F. Cut the squash in half lengthwise and scoop out the seeds. Brush the cut flesh with 1 to 2 tablespoons olive oil. Bake until tender, about 45 minutes.

Place the unpeeled garlic cloves on a square of aluminum foil. Drizzle with the remaining olive oil. Fold the foil around the garlic and seal. Bake for 25 to 30 minutes, until the garlic is soft.

Allow the squash to cool slightly then scoop out the pulp. Squeeze the roasted garlic cloves out of the skins. Put the squash and garlic through a ricer or purée in a food processor.

Heat the milk, butter, and thyme in a microwave or over low heat on the stove until the butter is melted and the milk very warm. Whisk the milk mixture into the puréed squash. Taste and add salt and pepper as needed.

Serves 4 to 6

roasted sweet potatoes
with red pepper-lime butter

Tender roasted sweet potatoes with melting red pepper-lime butter is a perfect dish to serve in the fall.

4 sweet potatoes, preferably orange-fleshed
1 red bell pepper, roasted, peeled, and diced
3 to 4 cloves garlic, chopped
1 to 2 Tbsp olive oil
1 tsp mild chili powder

¼ tsp ground cumin or to taste
1 stick butter, at room temperature or softened
Salt to taste
Juice of ½ lime or to taste

Cut the pepper into three or four nearly flat pieces. Place under a broiler, skin-side up. Cook until the skins are blistered and almost solidly black. Remove from the oven and place in a paper bag for at least 10 minutes. The skin will then peel off easily.

Preheat the oven to 375°F. Roast the sweet potatoes in the oven, in their skins, for about 40 minutes or until tender.

Meanwhile, make the red pepper-lime butter. Purée the roasted pepper with the garlic, olive oil, chili powder, and cumin in a blender or food processor. Remove from the processor and work in the soft butter by hand. Taste for seasoning, then add salt and lime juice as desired.

Serve this pepper butter spooned into each potato, or serve the sweet potatoes cut into thick slices with a piece of the flavored butter on top.

Serves 4

broccoli with feta, walnuts,
and red pepper

Walnuts and roasted red bell pepper dress up ordinary steamed broccoli. Cut the pepper into three or four nearly flat pieces. Place under a broiler, skin-side up. Cook until the skins are blistered and almost solidly black. Remove from the oven and place in a paper bag for at least 10 minutes. The skin will then peel off easily.

3 cups broccoli, including stems, cut up
2 Tbsp olive oil
⅓ cup chopped walnuts
1 Tbsp chopped fresh or 1 tsp dried basil

1 tsp lemon juice
1 roasted red bell pepper, peeled and diced
4 oz feta cheese, crumbled

Steam the broccoli until *al dente* (firm to the tooth).

Heat the oil in a large skillet. Add the walnuts and sauté for 1 minute over medium heat. Add the basil and sauté for 30 seconds. Add the broccoli and sauté for 2 minutes.

Remove the broccoli from the heat. Spoon the broccoli and walnuts into a serving dish. Add lemon juice and red pepper. Mix well. Add the feta cheese and serve.

Serves 4

oven-baked tomatoes

Baked tomatoes are too often regarded as a garnish rather than a serious vegetable, so here are some tips for making memorable baked tomatoes. Use tomatoes that are firm, not overripe. Time the cooking so you are ready to eat the tomatoes as soon as they come out of the oven. They don't keep well. Make your own crisp bread crumbs by toasting good bread, and grinding it coarsely, rather than using bland, finely ground commercial bread crumbs.

4 large tomatoes, firm but ripe
Salt
2 Tbsp olive oil
3 cloves garlic, minced
⅔ cup dried bread crumbs
2 Tbsp chopped fresh or 2 tsp dried basil
2 tsp chopped fresh or ½ tsp dried oregano
2 Tbsp minced scallion
⅓ cup Parmesan cheese

Preheat the oven to 425°F. Lightly grease a shallow baking pan.

Core the tomatoes and cut them in half. Lightly salt the cut sides, and place the tomatoes cut-side down on paper towels to drain while you prepare the topping.

Heat the oil in a small skillet. Add the garlic and sauté for 1 to 2 minutes, stirring and watching carefully so it doesn't scorch. If the oil is very hot, you may want to remove the pan from the burner. Add the bread crumbs, return the pan to the heat, and cook for 2 minutes, stirring almost constantly. Add the herbs and onion, cook for about 30 seconds, then remove the pan from the heat. Stir in the Parmesan cheese.

Place the tomatoes, cut-side up, in a lightly oiled baking pan. Divide the topping among the tomatoes. Bake at 425°F until the tomatoes lose their firmness but are not mushy, 15 to 20 minutes. Serve immediately.

Serves 4

roasted portobellos with pine nuts, peppercorns, and chervil

This delicious dish is easy to prepare. You may use large flat black mushrooms instead of portobellos if you like. If you do not have chervil, use fresh tarragon or chopped parsley and snipped chives.

4 portobello mushrooms or 12 large flat black mushrooms
5 cloves garlic, chopped
4 to 6 Tbsp extra-virgin olive oil, or to taste
2 Tbsp balsamic vinegar
Salt to taste
4 Tbsp pine nuts
1 to 2 tsp pink peppercorns or to taste
1 Tbsp chopped chervil

Arrange the whole mushrooms in a broiler pan or on a cookie sheet. Sprinkle with the garlic, olive oil, balsamic vinegar, and salt and allow to marinate for 30 minutes.

Meanwhile, lightly toast the pine kernels in a heavy-based, ungreased skillet, over medium-high heat, tossing every few moments, until the pine nuts are golden and lightly browned in spots. Remove from the heat and set aside.

Broil the mushrooms in their marinade, or bake in a 400°F oven, until they are browned on their gill sides. Then turn them over and cook until the outsides are lightly browned, about 10 to 15 minutes. Arrange the mushrooms on individual plates. Spoon over any juices, scatter over the pine nuts, pink peppercorns, and chervil and serve.

Serves 4

roasted potatoes in sweet hot sauce

This unusual potato dish will add character to any meal. The sauce derives its sweetness from the tomato and sugar, and its heat from fresh chiles.

1 onion, chopped
2 Tbsp olive oil
1 bay leaf
2 jalapeño or serrano chiles
2 tsp garlic, minced
1 Tbsp tomato paste
½ Tbsp sugar (up to 1 Tbsp, if the sauce is too tart)
1 Tbsp soy sauce
One 1-lb can plum tomatoes, chopped
⅔ cup white wine
Salt and black pepper
8 medium red potatoes

To prepare the sauce, gently cook the onions in the oil with the bay leaf. Mince the chiles. For a milder sauce remove the seeds and veins. When the onions are soft, add the chiles, garlic, tomato paste, sugar, and soy sauce. Cook for a further 5 minutes over low heat.

Add the chopped tomatoes and white wine. Stir and bring to a boil. Simmer for 10 minutes. Season to taste. This sauce should be slightly sweet; the flavor of the tomatoes should not dominate it.

To prepare the potatoes, cut into small cubes. Grease a cookie sheet. Season the potatoes well and brush with melted butter. Roast in a hot oven (450°F) until golden. Pour the tomato sauce over the potatoes and serve.

Serves 4

Left roasted portobellos with pine nuts, peppercorns, and chervil

spicy grilled vegetables

champ

Grilled squash, zucchini, eggplant, and fennel make an easy side dish when you're barbecuing the main course. Arrange them around the edges of the grill.

Sliced vegetables	Salt and pepper
Olive oil	
Paprika and ground cumin	
or other spices	

Slice squash, zucchini, eggplant, and fennel about ¼ inch thick. Zucchini and eggplant are attractive cut on the diagonal. Cut crooked-neck squash in half lengthwise.

Brush the cut edges lightly with olive oil and sprinkle with your favorite spices – paprika and cumin work well in this recipe, dried herbs do not. Lightly season with salt and pepper if you wish.

When the barbecue coals are no longer flaming, place the vegetables on the grill. Turn once during cooking: zucchini cooks quickly, about 5 minutes; eggplant takes 1 to 2 minutes longer; squash take about 10 minutes. The cooking times are a little shorter if the vegetables are directly over the coals instead of around the edges.

Garnish generously with chopped cilantro.

Serves 4

Right spicy grilled vegetables

A traditional Irish dish which combines creamy mashed potatoes and scallions. It is old-fashioned comfort food, made with plenty of milk and butter.

1¾ lb potatoes	⅔ cup rich milk
1 bunch scallions, about 8 to	Salt and black pepper
10, trimmed and sliced	1 stick butter

Peel the potatoes and cut them into small pieces. Bring to a boil in a pot of salted water, then cover and simmer for 15 to 20 minutes, until tender.

Meanwhile, simmer the scallions gently in the milk for 2 to 3 minutes until tender.

Drain the potatoes, then return them to the pot and place them over low heat for a minute or so, to allow any excess water to evaporate.

Add the milk and onions and pound or beat the potatoes to a soft, fluffy mash. Add plenty of salt and pepper as you go. Mound the champ in a large bowl. Make a hollow in the mound of potatoes for the butter and allow it to melt completely before serving.

Serves 4

sautéed spinach with ginger and macadamia nuts

fried coconut rice

Ginger, garlic, soy sauce, and macadamia nuts give spinach a whole new character in this easy dish.

2 lb fresh spinach, washed and trimmed	2 tsp grated ginger root
3 Tbsp vegetable oil	2 cloves garlic, minced
¼ cup chopped macadamia nuts	2 Tbsp soy sauce
	1 to 2 tsp rice wine vinegar

Bring water to a boil in a large pot. Have ready a large bowl of ice water. Blanch the spinach for 1 minute in the boiling water, then quickly remove it and plunge it into the bowl of ice water. This quick process preserves the bright green color of the spinach and keeps it from overcooking.

Drain the spinach well, then squeeze out as much moisture as possible. Transfer the spinach to a cutting board and chop it.

Heat the oil in a large skillet. Add the macadamia nuts. Sauté the nuts until they just begin to brown, about 1 minute. Add the ginger and garlic. Sauté about 30 seconds longer. Do not allow the garlic to brown.

Add the spinach and soy sauce, and sauté for a further 2 to 3 minutes, until the spinach is heated through. Remove from heat, splash with rice vinegar, and serve.

Serves 6

The addition of coconut milk to the water gives the rice a wonderful aroma and taste.

2 cups rice	1 clove garlic, minced
About 3 Tbsp sunflower or corn oil	1 cup thick coconut milk
1 small shallot, sliced	Salt

Measure out the required amount of rice, wash it, and drain thoroughly.

Pour enough oil into a saucepan to cover the base, about 3 tablespoons. Heat the oil and add the shallot and garlic. When they are becoming slightly golden, add the drained rice. Stir with a wooden spoon, frying the rice in the mixture.

Carefully pour in the coconut milk, then stir in 1 cup water. Add a pinch of salt. Bring the rice to a boil, lower the heat, and partially cover the saucepan.

When the liquid has evaporated to below the level of rice in the saucepan, remove the lid. With a chopstick make four or five holes in the rice to allow the liquid to evaporate completely. At this stage you should keep an eye on it to ensure it does not burn.

When the rice is nearly fully dry, remove from the heat. Ideally you should then let it settle for 20 minutes. Just before serving, fluff up the rice with a fork.

Serves 4

warm lentil and bacon salad

fried corn

Warm lentils, bacon, and onions are tossed in vinaigrette and sprinkled with parsley in this flavorful salad.

1 cup brown lentils, picked over for pebbles	1 cup chopped onion
	2 Tbsp red wine vinegar
1 small peeled onion, halved	⅓ cup olive oil
Several sprigs parsley	1 tsp Dijon-style mustard
2 bay leaves	1 clove garlic, minced
1 tsp salt	Pinch black pepper
1 tsp black pepper	1 tsp salt
3 slices bacon, diced	2 Tbsp chopped parsley

Bring four cups of water to a boil in a large saucepan. Add the onion halves, parsley, and bay leaves and simmer for 5 minutes. Add the lentils and cook until tender, 15 to 30 minutes. Discard onion, parsley, and bay leaves.

While the lentils are cooking, fry the diced bacon until crisp. Remove the bacon from the pan and set aside. Discard all but about 1 tablespoon of bacon fat. Reheat the remaining bacon fat and add the onions. Sauté for 5 minutes. Remove the onions and set aside.

Make the vinaigrette. Combine the vinegar, oil, mustard, garlic, pepper, and salt in a bottle and shake well to mix.

When the lentils are done, toss them in the vinaigrette and stir in the bacon and onion. Sprinkle with chopped parsley.

Serves 4

When there's an abundance of sweet, summer corn and you're looking for a change from corn on the cob – as simple and delicious as that is – try fried corn cooked in cream. You can use frozen corn, but it's better with fresh corn.

3 cups corn (4 to 5 ears)	1 tsp sugar
½ stick butter	½ tsp nutmeg
½ red bell pepper, diced	⅛ tsp cayenne
½ cup chopped scallions	Minced jalapeño chile to
½ cup heavy cream	taste (optional)

Cut the corn from the cob, then scrape the cobs with the dull edge of a knife to squeeze out any remaining milk.

Melt the butter in a skillet. Add the corn and corn milk, and cook over medium heat for 5 minutes, stirring frequently. Add the red pepper and scallions and the jalapeño, if desired, and cook for a further 2 minutes. Add the remaining ingredients. Cook for 3 minutes.

Serves 4

Fish glossary

BLUEFISH Bluefish is an oily, dark-fleshed, full-flavored fish with a fine, soft texture. It lives in warm waters other than the Pacific. Whole, it usually weighs between 3 and 5 pounds. Because of its oily flesh, its flavor gets stronger soon after it is caught, and it turns rancid quickly. It does not travel well and is best eaten where it is caught locally. Fillets have a thin strip of dark flesh where the fishy flavor – and any pollutants – are concentrated; the strip should be removed by cutting a shallow V along both sides and lifting it out. Bluefish can be cooked almost any way, and are particularly good grilled or stir-fried.

CATFISH Once a regional dish rarely seen outside the South, catfish have become so popular that they are farmed in commercial ponds throughout the United States, still mostly in the South. Farmed catfish, which typically weigh about 1 pound, are generally milder tasting than wild catfish, which have a slightly muddy flavor and may weigh up to 5 pounds or more. There are about 20 species of catfish, but channel catfish, a white-fleshed, firm-textured, medium-oily fish, is the most common commercial species. Catfish have a tough, inedible skin that must be removed. Frying is the most popular way of cooking catfish, but they also can be poached, steamed, grilled, baked, or sautéed.

COD More cod is eaten in the United States than any other finfish, and it is widely eaten throughout the world. Cod represents almost 10 percent of the world's total fish catch. It is fished in cold waters, mostly the North Pacific and North Atlantic. It has lean, medium-firm, snow-white flesh and a mild flavor. A whole fish can weigh 10 pounds or more. Small cod may be sold as scrod. Cod can be stuffed and baked whole, poached, braised, fried, and broiled, but does not grill successfully. Salt cod, which has been salted and dried, is soaked and reconstituted before eating. Salt cod is widely used in tropical countries because it keeps well and features in several Mediterranean dishes.

FLOUNDER The flounder, which includes most varieties of sole other than Dover sole, is a flatfish. Fine-grained, low in fat, and mild-flavored, it is one of the world's most popular fish. Most varieties weigh less than 5 pounds and include lemon sole, petrale sole, sand dab, plaice, butter sole, fluke or summer flounder, and yellowtail flounder. They are sold whole and as fillets. Flounder can be poached, baked, sautéed, steamed, broiled, and fried.

GROUPER There are hundreds of varieties of this warm-water fish, but the most common are the black, Nassau, red, and yellowfin grouper. Most whole fish sold in stores weigh 5 to 10 pounds, although they can be much larger. The grouper is often confused with the sea bass and can be used interchangeably in recipes. It has a firm, meaty texture, mild flavor, white flesh and is low in fat. It is usually sold whole or as fillets, and occasionally as steaks. Because of its firm texture, grouper can be grilled or cubed and make into kabobs, and can be cooked every way possible.

HADDOCK Haddock is closely related to cod and can be used interchangeably in recipes, but haddock is smaller, usually 2 to 5 pounds. The smallest haddock may be sold as scrod. Its flesh is lean, firm, white, and has a mild flavor. It is fished only in the North Atlantic; because of its popularity, its numbers off New England are declining. Haddock is usually sold as fillets, but may be found whole or as steaks. It can be cooked almost any way, including grilling. Smoked haddock is called Finnan haddie.

HALIBUT A favorite sport fish, the halibut lives in cold, deep water. It is most commonly associated with the North Atlantic and the waters off Alaska, although it may range as far south as the waters off Northern California. A related but inferior fish, the California halibut, can be fished off Southern California. The halibut is a giant flatfish, low in fat and with firm-textured flesh. It is usually sold as steaks, but some fish markets sell larger pieces for roasting.

Its weight usually ranges up to 60 pounds, although Alaskan halibut can weigh as much as 500 pounds. Halibut can be cooked almost any way, but may be dry when grilled or broiled.

MACKEREL The mackerel, which lives in the Atlantic Ocean off the North American and European coasts, is a firm-textured, oily-fleshed fish. Most varieties have strong flavors that pair well with assertive sauces, particularly sharp, fruit-based ones. The Spanish mackerel has a more delicate flavor; the wahoo or ono has a mild flavor and only a moderate fat content. Most mackerel available in retail stores are about 2 pounds and may be sold whole or filleted. Larger varieties, including the King and the wahoo, are also available as steaks. Mackerel is excellent on the barbecue because its high fat content keeps it moist. It is also good baked, broiled, and poached, and lends itself well to smoking.

MAHI MAHI Mahi mahi is the Hawaiian name for dolphin fish, though not the same as the dolphin mammal. Also known as dorado, Mahi mahi frequents the warm waters of the world. It has firm-textured flesh with a moderate fat content and dark flesh that turns white after cooking. Mahi mahi weighs up to 40 pounds, available mostly as steaks which can be cooked almost any way.

MONKFISH Also known as goosefish and angler fish, monkfish is notable for two things: its sheer ugliness and its sweet meat that is similar to lobster. The flavor is attributable to the fact that the monkfish eats mostly shellfish. Monkfish is mostly head; only the tail, which is sweet, mild, and meaty, is eaten. It is sold only as fillets, which can be grilled, sautéed, or cooked almost any way.

OCEAN PERCH Found in both the Atlantic and the Pacific, the ocean perch is a white-fleshed, firm-textured, low-fat fish with a mild flavor. It is almost always sold in fillets and is relatively inexpensive. Almost any method of cooking can be used.

POLLOCK The Atlantic pollock, also known as Boston bluefish, weighs about 4 to 12 pounds. It has a bluish cast, a firm texture, and is slightly oily. The Pacific pollock is white-fleshed, has a softer texture, and is low in fat. It is smaller than the Atlantic pollock, about 1 to 4 pounds, and is quite similar to cod, with which it can be used interchangeably. The slightly sweeter Pacific pollock is often used as imitation crabmeat. Both are most often sold as fillets and can be cooked by almost any method, although the Pacific pollock may not hold up as well on the barbecue.

POMPANO Pompano is a gourmet fish, delicious and usually expensive. It is found in the Atlantic Ocean along the southeastern coast of the United States, the Gulf Coast, and the Caribbean. Because of its small size – it rarely reaches 3 pounds – it is usually sold whole but may also appear as fillets. It is moderately fatty and firm-textured and barbecues well. It is excellent stuffed with crab, wrapped in foil, and baked whole, and can also be successfully pan-fried or grilled.

REDFISH Redfish is related to the Atlantic coast drum or croaker and the speckled trout of the Gulf of Mexico. It became so popular in the 1980s as Cajun blackened redfish that it is now scarce in Gulf waters, where fishing for it may be limited or prohibited. It is a low-fat, firm-textured fish. As substitutes, try sea bass, speckled trout, or croaker.

RED SNAPPER Red snapper is widely available along the Gulf of Mexico and Atlantic coasts. It is a low-fat, firm-textured fish with a mild flavor and vivid rose-colored skin. It is usually sold whole or as fillets. Filleted, red snapper can be substituted for redfish and blackened. It is an adaptable fish that can be cooked in a variety of ways, including baked, steamed, poached, broiled, grilled, fried, and sautéed.

ROCKFISH The plentiful rockfish is often sold as rock cod or Pacific snapper, although it is not related to the Atlantic's popular red snapper. There are more than 50 varieties of Pacific snapper, but they are generally low-fat, white-fleshed, firm-textured fish weighing 1 to 5 pounds with slightly sweet meat. They are sold as fillets and, less frequently, whole. The fillets can be cooked in almost any way except grilling; the whole fish barbecues well. The Hawaiian red snapper, also known as onaga, is often used in sashimi. Opakapaka is a Hawaiian pink snapper.

SALMON Salmon has richly flavored red or pink flesh that is high in fat. Pacific salmon range from San Francisco to the Arctic Circle, but most are Alaskan salmon. Unlike commercial Atlantic salmon, most of which are pen-reared, Pacific salmon are fished from the rivers of the North Pacific. The most popular Pacific varieties are the king or Chinook salmon, which usually ranges from 10 to 30 pounds but can be as large as 125 pounds, and the sockeye, which usually weighs about 6 pounds. Another type is the pink salmon, most of which is canned. Atlantic salmon, often called Norwegian salmon, are an endangered species, and wild Atlantic salmon cannot be sold legally in the United States. Salmon can be purchased whole, as fillets, or steaks. With its high fat content, it holds up well on the barbecue. It is delicious smoked or poached and eaten cold. Salmon also can be broiled, fried, baked, or steamed.

SEA BASS The black sea bass, from the North Atlantic, is the most common sea bass. It has a moderate fat content and a firm texture and is small — rarely more than 5 pounds. It is sold whole and as fillets, less frequently steaks. Black sea bass can be steamed, poached, baked, broiled, grilled, and pan-fried. The white sea bass, which grows to 40 pounds, is actually a member of the drum family. It can also be cooked by almost any method except pan-frying because of its size.

SHARK Shark steak, a less expensive alternative to the popular swordfish, is a firm, meaty, low-fat fish that is delicious grilled or used in kabobs. Most shark sold in restaurants or in fish markets is mako shark, and it is often sold as steaks. It is especially good marinated and barbecued, but also can be poached, steamed, roasted, broiled, and fried.

SKATE This fish, related to the shark, is shaped like a kite. A species of ray, by which name it is sometimes called, skate has a long, thick tail and winglike pectoral fins, which are the part that is eaten. The flesh is firm, low in fat, and white, with a delicate sweet taste, reminiscent of a scallop. Buy fillets with the tough skin already removed. Skate meat can be poached, grilled, broiled, steamed, sautéed, or deep-fried.

SWORDFISH The swordfish has a dense, meatlike texture and is caught in the temperate waters of the Pacific and Atlantic Oceans and the Gulf of Mexico. A whole swordfish typically weighs between 200 and 600 pounds or more. The flesh is dense and meaty, with a mild taste and moderate fat content. It is usually sold as steaks, which are delicious marinated and grilled on the barbecue. Swordfish is so versatile it can also be cut into chunks and threaded onto skewers for kabobs, broiled, poached, baked, sautéed, and steamed.

TILEFISH The tilefish, also called the tile bass, is a deep-water fish that is harvested from the Atlantic Ocean. It has firm white flesh and is low in fat. Fish range from 2 to 30 pounds in weight and may be sold whole, as fillets, and occasionally as steaks. Tilefish can be cooked by any method, including grilling.

TROUT The most common species of freshwater trout are rainbow, lake, brook, speckled, and golden trout. Wild trout have a wonderful flavor and rich, pink flesh. Most fish sold commercially is farm-raised, however, and lacks that rich flavor. A whole, one-pound trout (which produces about a half-pound of meat) is perfect for a single serving. The classic way of cooking it is to pan-fry it, preferably over an open fire. It is also good filleted and broiled, grilled (skin-side down only) over hot coals, stuffed and baked, poached, or roasted.

TUNA There are five major varieties of tuna, an oily, warm-water fish. The largest is the bluefin, which can weigh as much as 1,000 pounds. The smallest and least fatty is the bonito. Albacore is the only tuna that can be called white-meat tuna. The yellowfin, called ahi in Hawaii, has red flesh; the highest grade of yellowfin, with a deep red color and high fat content, is often used in sashimi. Skipjack, called ahu in Hawaii, has a bolder taste than ahi. Fresh tuna is almost always sold as steaks. It is delicious marinated and grilled over hot coals, with the inside still red like a good piece of beef. It also can be pan-fried, poached, or baked.

TURBOT The turbot is a flatfish with a mild taste, firm texture, and a low fat content. Turbot can weigh up to 25 pounds, although those under 10 pounds are more common. They are sold as fillets and occasionally as steaks, and can be poached, steamed, baked, broiled, sautéed, and fried.

Shellfish and squid glossary

CLAMS Hard-shell and soft-shell clams range from the tiny steamers and littlenecks to the huge geoduck, whose neck may protrude several feet from its shell, and giant sea clams, which can weigh several hundred pounds. The smallest clams are best for eating whole, usually steamed or in sauces. Bigger clams are usually tougher and are best minced, then added to sauces, chowders, and other dishes.

CRABS The species of fresh crab sold at your local fishmonger or grocer will depend largely on where you live, but meat from any type of crab will work in these recipes. Dungeness Crab, harvested from the San Francisco Bay to the Aleutian Islands and usually sold whole, generally weighs from 2 to 4 pounds and is large and meaty. Alaska's enormous king crab averages 10 pounds or more, with a leg span of 4 to 6 feet. The meat is snow-white with red edges and is mostly found in the legs, with relatively little in the body. The north Pacific's snow crab, about the size of the Dungeness, is known for its sweet flavor; it is usually sold in the form of frozen legs. The Blue Crab is harvested from Maryland

south and around the Gulf Coast of the United States. Usually sold by the barrel, the Blue Crab is small – it takes several to make a serving – but its meat is delicious. The Stone Crab is caught in the waters off Florida: its claws are removed and the body is thrown back into the sea, where it grows new claws. The claw is rock-hard but is full of sweet meat. It is usually eaten cold, dipped in a mustard sauce.

CRAWFISH Hugely popular in Louisiana's Cajun cooking and in Scandinavia, the crawfish is usually about 6 inches long. Usually sold whole, crawfish are boiled; the tail is twisted off the head and the tailmeat is eaten. Frozen tail meat can also be purchased and used in soups, sauces, and stuffings. Crawfish can be substituted for other shellfish in paella, cioppino, bisques, gumbo, jambalaya, and other dishes.

LOBSTER The lobster is the king of the crustacean family, and the most popular member of this royal family is the Maine lobster, which is found off the Atlantic coast of the Northern United States and Canada. Its relatives live in the waters off South Africa, Europe's Atlantic coast, and in the Mediterranean. The sweet meat is found in the tail and the claws. The spiny lobster or rock lobster, which lives in warmer waters, has only tailmeat and is not as sweet, but is also very popular. The simplest way to cook lobster is to boil it and serve it with melted butter and lemon, but lobster meat is also delicious in soups and salads.

MUSSELS Mussels are plentiful along the Pacific Coast, where they attach themselves to rocks and pilings along the beach. Most mussels are caught wild, but they are increasingly being farmed, from New Zealand to the Pacific Northwest. Sweet, tender California mussels are smaller than the most common Atlantic mussels; the sweet New Zealand green-lipped mussel is even larger. In Alaska, the wild blue mussel is considered a gourmet treat. Mussels can be steamed, barbecued, fried, baked, or used in soups, sauces, and dishes such as paella.

OYSTERS There are four major species of oysters: the Eastern, taken along the Atlantic seaboard; the Pacific, from Japan and the west coast of the United States; the Olympia, from Washington State's Puget Sound; and the European flat, sometimes called the Belon. Other names used – Chincoteague, Westcott, and so on – are based on their region of origin. Any fresh oyster will work in these recipes. They are typically eaten raw with a splash of lemon or hot pepper sauce, or battered in cornmeal and deep-fried. Oysters are also popular in soups and stews, grilled, and roasted.

SCALLOPS There are more than 400 species of scallops, but the three most common ones are the sea scallop, which is harvested in the North Atlantic and is the largest, at half an ounce to several ounces; the Bay scallop, harvested from the sea between Long Island and Massachusetts, which is smaller, has a more delicate flavor, and is the most expensive; and the Calico scallop, which grows in warmer waters, is tiny and overcooks and toughens quickly. Scallops are sold fresh and frozen. Very fresh, high-quality scallops are good in seviche. They also can be grilled, broiled, roasted, and sautéed, and can be used in soups and stews if added to the hot broth at the last minute so they do not overcook.

SHRIMP
Shrimp is the most popular shellfish in the United States and most of the world. They come in hundreds of species and almost as many colors and sizes, and may be wild or farmed. Generally, cold-water shrimp are smaller and more succulent than warm-water shrimp. Most shrimp are frozen before they are sold; the unfrozen shrimp in your market's display case are probably defrosted, not fresh. Price is usually determined by size – the larger the shrimp, the higher the price. Shrimp can be barbecued (preferably in the shell to prevent scorching), deep-fried, pan-fried, sautéed, boiled, or added to soups and stews at the last minute so they do not overcook.

SQUID Sometimes called by their Italian name, calamari, squid have a firm, chewy texture and a mild, slightly sweet taste. Squid can be bought fresh or frozen, whole, in steaks, or in rings. It should be cooked very briefly or simmered for a very long time to be tender. Otherwise that pleasant chewy texture will be tough and rubbery. In the United States, the most common way of cooking squid is to coat it in batter and deep-fry it. It can also be pan-fried, stir-fried, baked, or boiled. Squid can be added to soups, stews, and sauces, braised, or eaten raw in sushi.